KV-593-835

Partnerships
for Girls' Education

Oxfam GB

Oxfam GB, founded in 1942, is a development, humanitarian, and campaigning agency dedicated to finding lasting solutions to poverty and suffering around the world. Oxfam believes that every human being is entitled to a life of dignity and opportunity, and it works with others worldwide to make this become a reality.

From its base in Oxford in the United Kingdom, Oxfam GB publishes and distributes a wide range of books and other resource materials for development and relief workers, researchers and campaigners, schools and colleges, and the general public, as part of its programme of advocacy, education, and communications.

Oxfam GB is a member of Oxfam International, a confederation of 12 agencies of diverse cultures and languages, which share a commitment to working for an end to injustice and poverty – both in long-term development work and at times of crisis.

For further information about Oxfam's publishing, and online ordering, visit www.oxfam.org.uk/publications

For information about Oxfam's development, advocacy, and humanitarian relief work around the world, visit www.oxfam.org.uk

Partnerships
for Girls' Education

Edited by Nitya Rao and Ines Smyth

Oxfam

First published by Oxfam GB in 2005

© Oxfam GB 2005

ISBN 0 85598 513 5

A catalogue record for this publication is available from the British Library.

All rights reserved. Reproduction, copy, transmission, or translation of any part of this publication may be made only under the following conditions:

- with the prior written permission of the publisher; or
- with a licence from the Copyright Licensing Agency Ltd., 90 Tottenham Court Road, London W1P 9HE, UK, or from another national licensing agency; or
- for quotation in a review of the work; or
- under the terms set out below.

This publication is copyright, but may be reproduced by any method without fee for teaching purposes, but not for resale. Formal permission is required for all such uses, but normally will be granted immediately. For copying in any other circumstances, or for re-use in other publications, or for translation or adaptation, prior written permission must be obtained from the publisher, and a fee may be payable.

Available from:
Bournemouth English Book Centre, PO Box 1496, Parkstone, Dorset, BH12 3YD, UK
tel: +44 (0)1202 712933; fax: +44 (0)1202 712930; email: oxfam@bebc.co.uk

USA: Stylus Publishing LLC, PO Box 605, Herndon, VA 20172-0605, USA
tel: +1 (0)703 661 1581; fax: +1 (0)703 661 1547; email: styluspub@aol.com

For details of local agents and representatives in other countries, consult our website:
www.oxfam.org.uk/publications
or contact Oxfam Publishing, 274 Banbury Road, Oxford OX2 7DZ, UK
tel: +44 (0)1865 311 311; fax: +44 (0)1865 312 600; email: publish@oxfam.org.uk

Our website contains a fully searchable database of all our titles, and facilities for secure on-line ordering.

Cover image: Mashimoni Squatters primary school, Kenya (Geoff Sayer/Oxfam)

Published by Oxfam GB, 274 Banbury Road, Oxford OX2 7DZ, UK.

Printed by Information Press, Eynsham

Oxfam GB is a registered charity, no. 202 918, and is a member of Oxfam International.

Contents

Foreword

Cream Wright

This book provides a useful contribution to our understanding of the important topic of partnerships, which is rapidly becoming the most desirable as well as the most elusive variable in development work. Given the complex nature of partnerships and the current controversy surrounding the concept as a development 'buzz word', the contribution of this book needs to be placed in the context of the wider spectrum of issues and concerns relating to partnerships as a key factor in development work. In this regard we first need to distinguish between categories of partnership, at different levels, in order to increase our understanding of the issues involved.

At one level there is the broad category of partnership between governments and external agencies/organisations, usually designated as external development partners. At a second level there is the category of 'internal' partnerships between governments and national groups representing civil society, the private sector, and other special interests. At a third level there is the category of partnership between external partners seeking to assist countries in development. This might best be thought of as partnership within and between 'blocks' of external development partners, such as the multilateral agencies (mainly United Nations agencies), the international financial institutions (mainly development banks), the bilateral agencies, the global private sector (mainly multinational companies), and the international development foundations that represent private-sector or other special interests.

In addition to these three major levels and categories of partnership, there has also been a growing tradition of partnerships that link national groups directly with external partners. The links between international NGOs and national NGOs are probably the best illustration of this type. All these levels and categories of partnership are quite complex and challenging on their own, but new inter-relationships have emerged to complicate the field still further. For instance, there are new 'partnerships between partnerships', which require external agencies to work efficiently together as partners, in order to work more effectively in partnership with governments. In a similar vein, governments are increasingly required to work more effectively in partnership with national organisations in order to make more efficient use of the resources provided by external agencies as part of a new holistic partnership between a country and its external development partners. Generally then, as the contributions in this book indicate, partnerships have become increasingly complex and challenging as the drive for convergence and consolidation has intensified in an effort to build greater effectiveness and efficiency into development work at all levels.

There are a number of explanations for this increased emphasis on new ways of doing development work, which has in turn resulted in the growing importance of partnerships as a development imperative. First, as the number of external partners seeking to assist with development has increased, it has become obvious that there should be measures to avoid waste and duplication of efforts, as well as to reduce the high transaction costs to governments of servicing such a plethora of external assistance initiatives. Second, it has also become apparent that the main mode of providing external assistance in the form of development projects has severe limitations. Projects typically provide tied resources for achieving specific objectives within specified time frames. In this regard, even successful projects may leave unattended critical needs which are essential for development but were not part of the original project. They may also cause other areas of cross-sectoral work to be marginalised, while resources and attention are concentrated on project areas. In addition, projects tend to monopolise expertise and drain national capacity with their servicing requirements, which are not necessarily linked to the mainstream of capacity building for development. As a result, there has been a shift towards doing development work in a manner that strengthens national capacity, deals more broadly with the various sectors, makes inter-sectoral connections, and provides resources in a more flexible and reliable manner for development. Third, the tendency for external concerns and priorities to dominate external assistance has been viewed as counter-productive for development work. This has produced a shift towards clustering development efforts around central concerns and priorities that are defined by the countries themselves (governments with participation by other stakeholders), rather than by external development partners. These shifts and changes in emphasis point to the need for all development stakeholders to work closely with each other in collaborative patterns that promote greater synergy, improved efficiency, and increased effectiveness. In a word, partnership has become the name of the game in development work!

Some of the consequences of these new ways of doing development are still unfolding, but we know enough to appreciate that partnerships are much more complex than the theoretical constructs and principles suggest. For instance, it seems clear that successful partnerships depend not simply on what the partnership is about and who the partners are, but also on why the partnership is being established, what is the power relationship between the partners, how much (and what) each partner is prepared to lose and gain as a result of the partnership, and what each partner has to offer or expects to receive from the partnership. These indicate quite clearly that partnerships are not only about principles, technical strategies, and operational arrangements. They are more importantly about the 'politics' and perceptions of each agency, in terms of its own competencies, comparative advantages, and mandates, as they relate to other agencies, the sector in question, and the country involved. Given such complexity, it is best to try to understand partnerships from within a single sector or development theme. This is another advantage of this book, in that it concentrates its analysis of partnerships within the area of girls' education as one of the key development priorities.

The book recognises and highlights the fact that all key stakeholders have invested considerable 'agency capital' in reaching a remarkable global consensus on development priorities, as reflected in the Millennium Declaration and the Millennium Development

Goals (MDGs), which most countries have agreed to strive to achieve. This consensus also extends to various sectoral priorities such as the Education for All (EFA) Dakar Goals and various conventions such as the Convention on the Rights of the Child (CRC) and the Convention on Elimination of all Forms of Discrimination Against Women (CEDAW). All of these have a bearing on the theme of girls' education that is the focus of this book. This theme draws together stakeholders with an interest in education as well as those dealing with gender issues and concerns for social/economic equality. The theme of girls' education therefore brings together a wide range of partners from within the education sector as well as from other key sectors and some with cross-sectoral concerns. On the one hand, then, there have been unprecedented achievements in agreeing global targets for development. On the other hand, there is the main challenge highlighted in the book: how to make partnerships the reality that can help to translate these investments into development dividends for countries and their partners.

Efforts to translate these consensus investments into development dividends have unleashed a range of initiatives and processes which increasingly dominate the development landscape. For instance, the United Nations Reform Process now obliges UN agencies in many countries to do a Common Country Assessment (CCA) that will form the basis of a United Nations Development Assistance Framework (UNDAF), within which UN agencies will provide assistance to countries. The bilateral agencies are increasingly moving towards sector-wide processes such as the Fast Track Initiative, through which external development partners will provide support to countries based on a national plan and with funding that goes into the government's budget or is generally available for sectoral expenditures on a flexible basis.

As these initiatives and processes take root, it is becoming evident that the critical question is how to build partnerships that can utilise the ensuing benefits as part of a process of building even greater synergy and focus around agreed priorities, and with greater efficiency and effectiveness for the whole process of development. How do we get the UN reform process to link in with Fast Track Initiative and other sector-wide processes? The danger is that each of these initiatives and processes can very easily become an all-consuming entity in its own right, raising partnership issues all over again, but at a higher level. Are sector-wide approaches currently being dominated by the major bilaterals, not withstanding the rhetoric about country leadership? Are these sector-wide processes really inclusive, or largely restricted to 'funding' agencies? Do they deprive countries of the full benefits that could be derived from a 'total resource package' provided by a more inclusive range of partners, rather than just funding agencies? How do we ensure that multiple voices relating to a variety of legitimate development concerns are meaningfully represented within these initiatives and processes? For instance, why has it taken so long for issues relating to HIV/AIDS and to gender (girls' education) to be factored into the Fast Track Initiative? What do we need to do about the specific needs and rights of disadvantaged families and communities while waiting for these system-wide initiatives and processes to make an impact? What happens to the valuable development lessons that have been learned through projects and grassroots work, when the development process becomes dominated by systems-related concerns?

It is against this background of myriad questions relating to these new ways of doing development that the type of thematic partnership addressed in this book becomes highly relevant for our understanding of the tensions and possibilities of partnerships. There are various partnerships at all levels relating to girls' education as a gender-equitable development theme, and the task for all such partnerships appears to be two-fold. First is the need to ensure that the right of girls (as well as boys) to access and complete a good-quality basic education remains in focus and is strongly facilitated by all stakeholders. Second is to put the concerns relating to girls' education into the new initiatives and processes with an appropriate level of priority. It is clear that if these tasks are to be adequately addressed, then the various partnerships for girls' education need to be moulded into a much more coherent and influential movement for girls' education.

The experience with the United Nations Girls' Education Initiative (UNGEI) is discussed at various points in the book. UNGEI is very much a work in progress; but, from the perspective of UNICEF as the lead agency, the experience to date already suggests some partnership issues and strategies that can contribute to the way forward. First, it is clear that partners within UNGEI have diverse priorities that have drawn them towards support for girls' education. These include promoting access to quality education for all children, strengthening female reproductive-health issues, improving the conditions of the disadvantaged in society, combating HIV/AIDS, and eliminating child labour. Despite this variety of priority concerns, there is clearly a vested stake in girls' education as a means of delivering results on all these priorities. It is also clear that different partners have their own comparative advantage to offer for a stronger partnership, and that all partners have something that is of value to the cause. Increasingly, therefore, the challenge for UNGEI is to make effective use of such comparative advantage that its partners have to offer and to build synergy for work on girls' education out of the total movement. There are partners who are best at providing examples and guidance on good practice. There are partners who are best at working with countries to scale up these good practices to national level. There are partners with a comparative advantage in helping countries to make major changes in their patterns of investment in education and related areas. There are others who can best contribute by accompanying countries through the difficult phase of implementing major changes and reforms in their education systems. All are a valuable part of a strong partnership for girls' education. For them to work in harmony, it may be necessary for partner agencies to revise their perceptions of each other and come to a better understanding of the positive politics involved in 'working smart' through making use of comparative advantages in a co-ordinated manner. This is the direction in which UNICEF and other partners envisage UNGEI moving at the country level, as well as at regional and global levels, as it tries to engage much more constructively with the new initiatives and processes in education and development.

The value of this book is that it reveals some of the tensions with which an ambitious partnership like UNGEI would have to contend in building synergy and co-ordinating efforts in support of girls' education, and in developing its ability to deliver on the many promises that gave rise to such a partnership in the first place.

Cream Wright
Education Chief, UNICEF

Acronyms and abbreviations

AA	ActionAid
ADEA	Association for the Development of Education in Africa
AGEI	African Girls' Education Initiative
AIDESEP	Inter-ethnic Association for the Development of the Amazon
BRAC	Bangladesh Rural Advancement Committee
CAMPE	Campaign for Education
CBO	community-based organisation
CCNGO	Collective Consultation on NGOs in EFA and Literacy
CoE	Centre of Excellence
CMES	Centre for Mass Education in Science
CSO	civil-society organisation
DAM	Dhaka Ahsania Mission
DFID	Department for International Development
DNFE	Directorate of Non-Formal Education
EFA	Education For All
EGEI	Egypt Girls' Education Initiative
EI	Education International
FAWE	Forum for African Women Educationalists
FEMSA	Female Education in Mathematics and Science in Africa
FTI	Fast Track Initiative
GCE	Global Campaign for Education
GEM	Girls' Education Movement
GPU	Government of Bangladesh Partnership Unit
INGO	international non-government organisation
MDG	Millennium Development Goal
MINEDAF	Ministers of African Education

MoE	Ministry of Education
NAP	National Action Plan
NCCM	National Council for Childhood and Motherhood
NCEFA	National Committee on Education For All
NFE	non-formal education
NEPAD	New Partnership for Africa's Development
NER	net enrolment rate
NGO	non-government organisation
OI	Oxfam International
PRSP	Poverty Reduction Strategy Paper
SSA	sub-Saharan Africa
TWG	Technical Working Group
UCEP	Underprivileged Children's Education Programme
UNGEI	United Nations Girls' Education Initiative
WCEFA	World Conference on Education For All

Acknowledgements

The editors wish to thank Janice Dolan (Oxfam GB), Carol Watson (UNICEF), and Ellen Van Kalmthout (UNICEF) for their perceptive and constructive comments on early drafts of this book.

Introduction: principles and realities

Nitya Rao and Ines Smyth

Since 1990, the United Nations has sponsored a series of world summits and laid the foundation for a comprehensive development agenda which includes goals related to education, health, social development, and gender equality, with time-bound targets and quantified indicators. The goals are summarised in the Millennium Development Goals (MDGs), adopted by the UN General Assembly in June 2001. In the case of education, the MDGs confirmed the intent and timetable set by the World Education Forum, in Dakar, Senegal, in 2000, enshrined in the Dakar Framework for Action. They include '*the elimination of gender disparities in primary and secondary education (preferably) by 2005 and at all levels by 2015*' (Target 4, Goal 3). This book seeks to contribute to the achievement of the goal of gender-equitable education, by reflecting on the experiences of various forms of partnership, their achievements and challenges.

During the 1990s, girls' primary-school enrolment improved in all regions of the developing world. However, differences persist within countries and across regions. Out of the 128 countries that have been monitoring progress in terms of gender parity in education, 54 still display strong disparities in favour of boys. This is particularly the case in Central and West Africa, South and West Asia, and some of the Arab States (UNESCO 2003). In countries such as Ethiopia, Niger, Pakistan, and Chad, enrolment ratios for girls are as low as two-thirds of those for boys. Only 18 among these countries have a realistic chance of achieving the gender-parity goal by 2005 – or even by 2015. For the others, the goal cannot be achieved unless specific and extremely vigorous initiatives are put in place.

Apart from enrolment, the position of girls and women in education is reflected in the relative rates of school drop-out and repetition, of completion and achievement. In the past ten years, the global focus has been on primary schooling, but disparities are particularly visible in the transition to secondary education. For example, in East Asia, while gender parity has generally been achieved at the primary level, the gender gap in secondary education is as wide as 13 per cent in favour of boys in Cambodia, 12 per cent in Laos, and 9 per cent in Indonesia and China (Hyde and Miske 2001:8). Of the 862 million illiterate adults in the world, two-thirds are women (UNESCO 2002).

These disparities justify the global consensus on the compelling need to enhance girls' education and promote gender-equitable education, especially in those countries where the gender gaps are wide, in order to provide girls and boys with equal opportunities and life choices. This consensus is reflected in current moves among donors and international agencies towards greater co-ordination and partnership, through the Fast Track Initiative for education (launched at the IMF–World Bank meetings in 2002), sector-wide approaches (SWAps), general budget support to national governments, and – with specific reference to girls' education – through the UN Girls' Education Initiative (UNGEI). These measures are intended to enhance a sense of national 'ownership' of education reforms. They mark a shift from a strategy of offering one-off support to individual projects to a strategy of providing integrated programmatic support, based on the recognition that universal and equitable education requires multi-dimensional and multi-sectoral interventions. At the national level, the equivalent has been an attempt to involve civil society and private organisations in State-led educational interventions. Hence the growing interest in partnership to achieve the goals of Education For All, agreed at the World Conference on Education For All, held in Jomtien, Thailand, in 1990.

However, as King has suggested, the 'new partnership paradigm may not remove selectivity or indirect conditionality', because rich donor countries retain the right to choose partners in accordance with their own criteria (1999: 16). In her analysis of the Fast Track Initiative, Rose (2003) similarly found that the preconditions for partnership were likely to leave the poorest countries without additional funding for achieving their education goals. One must, moreover, remember that different organisations may have different justifications for conforming to the consensus: from purely instrumental arguments which advance the economic reasons to increase human capital (World Bank 2002) to those that emphasise human rights and empowerment (Heward 1999). How far are such major players willing to suppress their individual identities and interests? We shall return to these ideological differences in the next section, where we reflect on the current emphasis on partnerships in development.

Understanding partnerships

This book documents the creation of partnerships to promote girls' education, pointing to a great diversity of experiences, forms, and outcomes. It identifies key elements for successful partnerships, as well as the problems and pitfalls encountered in reality. The purpose of the exercise is to encourage all stakeholders to consider whether simply adhering to a shared notion of the importance of girls' education will by itself guarantee the achievement of the

2005 and 2015 goals. In the words of the UN Special Rapporteur of the Commission on Human Rights, commenting on the right to education,

> *Since the Jomtien Conference in 1990, globalised policy-making has replaced the conventional state-centred system, with a new vocabulary reflecting that change. The focus on the grand and fuzzy is exemplified in terms such as* mainstreaming *or* partnership; *defining a common position came down to seeking the lowest common denominator in platitudinous declarations.*

(Tomasevski 2003:3)

It may be helpful at this stage to review the notion of partnerships in development in a historical context, and consider the nature of the players involved in the field of education.

Different actors in development

The debate about partnerships began in the development arena in the context of debates about the role of the State versus that of other institutions. During the first and second UN 'development decades' (the 1950s and 1960s), the State was seen to have primary responsibility for economic growth, the elimination of poverty, and provision of basic services, in much of the post-colonial, developing world. But the State came under severe attacks, on one side from a progressive perspective which mistrusted control by elite groups lacking commitment to the poor, and on the other side from a neo-liberal perspective which saw the State as inefficient and corrupt. As Mackintosh puts it: 'Disillusionment with the state produced for a time agreement – on the need to reduce its power, decentralise its operations and devolve some of its activities, including decisions on use of state funds to non-state bodies' (1992:87).

From the 1970s onwards, this tendency encouraged the growth of both civil society and market institutions.[1] Yet these three sectors – the State, the market, and civil society – functioned at this time in distinct domains. As Korten (1990) has shown, governments, with their ability to exercise coercive power, were seen as more suited to maintaining basic law and order and providing security to all citizens; the advantage of the business or market sector was seen to lie in its economic power, while the advantage of the voluntary sector was perceived to be its commitment to moral values and its capacity for social and institutional innovation in response to the needs of the politically and economically disenfranchised.

In the 1980s, a change took place in the relationships between these institutions, for several reasons. One concerns developments within civil society.[2] While non-government organisations (NGOs) had been engaged in considerable innovative work at the local level (described by Fowler [1988] as their 'comparative advantage'), they somehow seemed unable to make the link between their work at the grassroots and the wider systems and structures that formed the institutional context of their work. A need arose to assess their impact and to consider the strategic choices open to them if they were serious about enhancing their impact (Edwards and Hulme 1992). In the process, observers recognised the diversity within the NGO/civil-society sector. Edwards (2000) identifies the possible role for NGOs as service providers, but equally sees potential roles for them as protectors of human rights, defenders of the independence of lobby groups, supporters of dynamic communications media, and promoters of citizens' education and the organisation of workers.[3]

A second reason for the relational change is associated with the growing processes of globalisation in the 1980s and 1990s, with two connected challenges for NGOs. The first links back to the seeming impossibility of enhancing their impact in isolation from national and international political process. Second, with the scaling-back of State provisioning, in accordance with the IMF–World Bank conditionalities, a need arose for alternative service providers.

Until the 1980s, NGO–State relationships had usually been distant, but the pressure on NGOs to scale up their impact made it necessary to find ways for more active engagement with the State and other actors in the larger development context. This pressure was further strengthened by the 'good governance' agenda promoted by the multilateral and bilateral donors. Popularly known as the 'Washington Consensus', the idea of 'good governance' emphasises an economic order based on free markets, a minimal 'enabling role' for the State, and the participation of civil society in decision making. In the 1990s, the notion of corporate social responsibility also encouraged links between NGOs and business establishments.

In the past few years, there has been some reversal in this trend. Doubts are being expressed about the legitimacy of the market to deliver basic services and about its assumed superiority in meeting development goals. Equity in 'starting conditions' is essential for markets to work, and letting markets loose in an imperfect world has served only to produce more inequality. Hence the need to 'bring the State back in'. In its *World Development Report 1997*, the World Bank observes: 'The message of experience since then is rather different: that the state is central to economic and social development, not as a direct provider of growth but as a partner, catalyst, and facilitator' (World Bank 1997:1). For NGOs and civil society, democratic states, rather than unregulated free markets, provide an environment that is more supportive of people-oriented development and offers a greater opportunity for poor communities to demand accountability from policy makers and service providers. It is also important to note that the State is not a monolithic entity: it represents a diversity of interests and ideologies. While progressive policy commitments may exist, the manner of their implementation varies across sectors and levels of operation; alliances with supportive bureaucrats and politicians play a key role in moving agendas forward. Finally, it should be acknowledged that while the superiority of the market is being questioned in theory, in practice the private sector has a past record of involvement in charitable work, and has more recently made considerable inroads into social-sector activities previously reserved to the State.

Although much of the development debate has focused on the respective roles and merits of the State, the market, and civil society, the presence of another set of actors cannot be ignored: that of bi-lateral and multilateral agencies. Such agencies are often characterised in generic terms as 'donors', but their nature, mandates, resources, and reach make them diverse and usually powerful stakeholders in development in their own right. The importance of such agencies, and especially the international financial institutions, is often noted in comparison with the relative powerlessness of certain States, especially in Africa. Critiques of the role that they play in development concern the well-rehearsed problem of (lack of) aid coherence across countries and sectors, alongside their undermining of national sovereignty and ownership. Assistance to poor countries on the basis of numerous disparate 'projects', funded by a multitude of donor governments, is often of doubtful impact, and undermines the already limited control exercised by recipient governments over such initiatives. The recognition of these problems led to the emergence of the Sector Wide Approach by donor governments.[4] The MDGs too are a reflection of the UN's aspiration to prioritise a global development agenda and seek greater co-ordination and harmonisation at all levels to achieve it.

Given the profound differences in functions, power, and goals among the various development actors, the word 'partner' can thus be interpreted in many different ways – as *collaborator, contractor, supporter, client, patron* (Fowler 2000a: 3). It is not surprising then that notions of partnership which on paper seem simple and attractive are not easy to realise in practice.

The new partnership paradigm

Recent development debates reveal a growing concern with the terminology and the practice of 'partnership'. According to the World Bank: 'Governments need to build partnership with the private sectors, NGOs, assistance agencies and the organizations of civil society to define development needs and implement programs' (2000:21). What is new is the fact that partnership is now explicitly perceived as instrumental to the achievement of the Millennium Development Goals. According to Helmich, 'if the objective of reducing by 50 per cent the number of people living in poverty by the year 2015 is to be achieved, one key factor should be a co-ordinated approach to address the needs of those living in poverty in the South' (1999:3).

As we have observed, while the evolution of the partnership discourse has given rise to a wealth of new and interesting ideas, the practice has been more complex and problematic. Even within the World Bank's own Poverty Reduction Strategy Paper (PRSP) process, participation in terms of wide consultation with a range of stakeholders has been sought at the initial stages of poverty assessment, but this has not necessarily been followed through once the strategy is finalised and being implemented. This is the case in all fields and sectors, including that of education. The themes of this book – as summarised below – reflect on the implications of various forms of partnerships for education, and in particular for those interventions that are aimed at promoting girls' education.

Contributors to this book illustrate the vast array of alliances and partnerships that currently exist, some of which have emerged only recently. In some contexts NGOs might work as service contractors for the State, as in the provision of non-formal education in Bangladesh; others might be involved in grassroots organising outside the domain of the State or donors. Here too partnerships may be formed, but in this case they link NGOs and people's movements, as in the Philippines in the early 1990s (Constantino-David 1992), as well as in the present education networks. Another configuration of partnership is that between Southern and Northern NGOs and people's movements, as in the struggle for better resettlement for those displaced by the Itaparica Dam in Brazil (Hall 1992). A more recent example is that of the Global Campaign for Education – a partnership between NGOs, academic bodies, and teachers' unions – established to lobby for achieving the educational commitments made at Dakar. Private-sector organisations are not absent. For example, in the UK, profit-seeking organisations are contracted by the government to provide a range of services in education. In developing countries, for-profit organisations appear to be found mostly in local-level collaborations with NGOs.

In this book we consider this trend in relation to three sets of related issues: first, the need to acknowledge differences in power and resources among the various actors; second, the risk that flexibility to function as equal partners may be restricted by procedures and structures within different organisations, and by the fear of loss of identity; and finally the question of whether the partnerships that are being created can be successfully scaled up in size and supported to become self-sustaining.

Power relations

A key problem in the partnership discourse (Fowler 2000b) is that it disguises the fact that power differences exist, and inequality is not likely to be eradicated without friction. In many ways, the discourse on partnership mirrors the discourse on social capital, in which associations and networks are seen to enhance trust and consequently improve development outcomes. Writers such as Harriss (2000), Fine (1999), and Prakash and Selle (2004) have pointed out that the language of social capital both depoliticises and decontextualises development, by ignoring the power relations between different groups. A similar tendency seems to be the case with the language of partnerships.

Depending on the actors involved, the issue at hand, and the prevalent context, with all its diversity and risk, the nature of the 'partnership' is likely to vary (Lewis and Wallace 2000), but what remains constant is the existence of unequal power relations. As Elu and Banya note, 'Poverty in the south is an ominous backdrop to the practice of true partnership and institutional development' (1999:194). Financial dependence of Southern governments and NGOs on the North creates a context where the latter can more easily play a dominant role within the partnership. Similarly, in most developing countries, 'the state is all-powerful, and voluntary organisations must operate carefully vis-à-vis the state' (ibid.: 195). The lack of financial resources is a major factor which perpetuates unequal relations within partnerships at all levels. As Lake and Mugwendere point out in this book, the provision of financial security through education subsidies is often a necessary measure in the creation of community alliances.

A second problem, identified by Howell and Pearce (2000), is that the partnership approach assumes value consensus and a common vision. On the contrary, these are often absent or problematic in particular cultural and political contexts. In Central and Latin America, civil society emerged as part of a radical political agenda of grassroots movements opposed to military regimes; but these agendas are not reflected in the funding packages from external donors in the region. In Guatemala, for instance, funding is often directed towards certain types of NGO which promote a liberal democratic agenda, at the expense of more radical groups. The chapter from the Philippines included in this book illustrates this point. Howell and Pearce further argue that donors' attempts to strengthen civil-society partnerships have in fact led to the imposition of a particular vision of civil society and of partnerships, blunting the political potential of such organisations. This emerges from the evidence (cited by King 1999) of donors selecting particular kinds of NGO and government: those that are willing to comply with their priorities and agendas.

A related danger is that of co-option. Especially for NGOs and civil-society groups, forming partnerships requires them to be conscious of the dangers of 'standardisation' between their own policy and practice and that of donors or governments. While the State may welcome NGOs' welfare work, it may not favour their critiques of its official policies. Similarly, business interests may sponsor community development projects, but react against demands for minimum labour standards and environmental standards. Trying to adapt to these pressures may lead to co-option as well as the loss of political edge.

Profound differences in ideology can prevent meaningful collaboration. For instance, within the Global Campaign for Education (GCE) there are disagreements about the relative priorities that should be accorded to teachers' interests and those of poor communities. If not managed, these conflicts may lead to a failure of the partnership itself. (See Patrick Watt's chapter in this book.)

The contrary is also true: a shared ideology can help to mitigate inequalities. The closer the members of coalitions and alliances are in terms of their values and ethos, the smoother their functioning promises to be, as indicated in Adaeze Igboemeka's chapter on a major network of donors. Holding common values can also provide the impetus and energy to promote novel programmes, as discussed in the case study from Peru contributed by Sheila Aikman. Her chapter also traces the transformation of the policy makers' agenda from a focus on access to formal education to a more robust questioning of the quality and relevance of schooling, and the need for indigenous control over decisions about curriculum, language policy, and pedagogy.

Flexibility

As development donors gradually shift from being allies or supporters of national governments and civil society to being 'partners' in their initiatives, the depth and breadth of the relationship increase. At times, however, the rhetoric is stronger than the reality. Recognising the different goals and commitments of different actors, as well as their differing institutional systems and structures, can help to anticipate the problems that may emerge in forging strong alliances.

A first set of problems might relate to the reluctance of organisations to give up or share with others what they perceive as their core responsibilities and legitimate role, because they feel that in some ways their capacity and credibility are being challenged. In this book, Ahmadullah Mia presents an example from Bangladesh, where the government is reluctant to recognise NGO schools as 'proper' primary schools and NGO training centres as legitimate training institutions. There is then a struggle over content and curriculum, with the State retaining the final authority, refusing to involve local communities or even civil society in this process, and granting recognition only to those who adopt the State-approved curriculum. In the Philippines, as we see in the chapter contributed by Rene Raya and Raquel dG. Castillo, issues of institutional identity, visibility, and interests make it difficult to establish functioning partnerships.

Added to this is the likely shift in political attitudes and spaces for partnership when changes occur in political regimes and leadership. Committed leadership, however, has played a major role in closing gender gaps in education, as we see in the case study from Egypt (contributed by Malak Zalalouk) and the example of the Forum for African Women Educationalists (presented by Penina Mlama).

There is clearly a tension between the pressure to combine a range of methods and forms of education provision through partnerships, and the need to retain one's institutional identity and clearly defined role. The solution often lies in dividing responsibilities and tasks among partners, according to their capacities and experience, to enhance complementarities rather than competition. While in the abstract this is a good strategy, at present the division of responsibilities seems to be decided on terms dictated by governments. In most of our examples, formal education is the domain of the State, and the sphere of non-formal education is almost entirely an NGO preserve. Such separation might build on the relative strengths of partners, but it can create a dualism in terms of the valuation of different kinds of educational provision. So, while formal, State-provided education is seen as the norm, non-formal NGO provision is seen somehow as second-class, meant for the poor and marginalised. The situation, however, is negotiable rather than fixed. For example, in Bangladesh as a result of sustained NGO negotiation, children from NGO-run 'non-formal' schools can now seek admission to 'formal', government-run secondary schools.

Institutional structures are as important as values in determining the nature and the success of partnerships. Recognising and confronting such differences, rather than pretending that they do not exist, appears to be the best strategy. Openness to the principle of shared decision-making, long-term commitment to shared programmes, and developing mutually acceptable goals and standards gives hope for developing 'partnerships'.

Scaling up and sustainability

Scaling up local interventions and helping them to become sustainable are often mentioned as desirable in development. The discourse of partnerships in education contains several aspects relating to sustainability.

The first concerns ownership. According to the current development orthodoxy, a major reason for project failure is the lack of ownership and involvement by all the actors, especially local communities. Communities will not maintain the assets and benefits created through such a partnership unless they are involved in the planning process and not only in the implementation phase. In other words, sustainability is possible if communities 'own' projects. Yet, in analysing community participation in education, Subrahmanian (2004) notes that this has often increased women's work burdens, because women provide more of the community support than men do. Development projects, however, can achieve substantial cost reduction for the implementing agencies by involving communities in a partnership.

Second, with the underlying acceptance of the State's primary role in education provision comes an emphasis on close collaboration with governments and the need to support the implementation of national policies. Partnerships such as the donor network discussed by Igboemeka in this collection can then become successful by providing technical assistance and support to governments, rather than to independent projects.

Another aspect of sustainability is the importance of strong leadership within the government. Efforts to achieve gender equity in education become sustainable as a result of long-term personal commitment and initiative of the top leadership, as illustrated through the examples presented by Zaalouk, Murage, and Mia, rather than a general statement of national commitment.

The Egyptian example raises a further point: concrete and lasting results from the programme described were obtained thanks to the mediation role of UNICEF, an external and neutral agency. The long-term dialogues established by UNICEF assisted the formation and maintenance of partnerships between communities, NGOs, and government – entities essentially asymmetrical and at times incompatible. The Campaign for Female Education (CAMFED, described here by Lucy Lake and Angeline Mugwendere) seems to play a similar mediating role, establishing links between communities, countries, and individuals across Africa. Whether the potential for this initiative to be scaled up will be realised depends on the openness to innovation on the part of donors and other stakeholders, and their willingness to invest considerable resources in building community institutions and alliances.

Another key lesson emerging from several chapters in this book is the need for effective communication and co-ordination, as well as building the capacity of partners in order to ensure sustainability and facilitate scaling-up. But this is a costly process, which requires the investment of resources.

To conclude, scaling up appears most realistic when a partnership involves members who have the capacity and commitment to learn from practice and disseminate lessons, and others who have positions and resources that allow such lessons to be applied elsewhere and on a larger scale. Sustainability comes from individual creativity and long-term personal commitment, backed by institutional mechanisms and resources. It cannot rely on voluntarism alone.

Lessons learned from partnerships in other fields

Despite the complexities and problems inevitably encountered in the practice of partnership in education, it should be stressed that there are useful precedents from which we can learn lessons. Environment-conservation movements and women's movements have demonstrated the strength of partnership to drive social change. A further example comes from the women's health movement, in which there has been considerable shift and progress in policies and attitudes, particularly on the matter of reproductive health. This experience is worth analysing for the lessons that it may offer to organisations that are currently engaged in efforts to change attitudes and policies concerning girls' education.

In earlier decades, mainstream thinking and programmes on reproductive health mainly focused on trying to alter the demographic profile of communities and the reproductive behaviour of women, in an attempt to stem what was seen as a 'population explosion' in developing countries (Tremayne 2001). The Cairo International Conference on Population and Development in 1994 marked a shift to a concern with reproductive health and women's rights: the Programme of Action advocated quality of services, gender equality, and the empowerment of women.

There is evidence to show that civil society in the North and in the South was instrumental in bringing about this shift: '…the NGO involvement in the Cairo Conference resulted in the international recognition of women's concerns and women's rights as human rights. It became clear that NGOs are an intellectual, political and social force to be reckoned with, possessing valuable expertise for the development of policies that are more responsive to women's needs' (Holzner, Kollmann, Darwisyah 2002:1).

In particular it was the women's movement and health movements and their organisations in the South that came together to bring about these transformations. But to what extent was such a success attributable to partnerships among actors? In many developing countries, advocates did establish important alliances with staff of bilateral and multilateral organisations, and with government departments (Dixon-Mueller 1993). Yet many analysts are critical of the limited extent to which governments responded to the call by the Beijing Platform of Action[5] to work with NGOs (WEDO 1998). Further, competition among women's organisations has prevented effective collaboration and partnership, often to the detriment of smaller and less sophisticated NGOs (Holzner et al. 2002).

There is thus no absolute consensus on whether changes in policies, attitudes, and language on reproductive health are indeed positive. Some organisations see the 'Cairo consensus' as the 'co-optation of women's powerful critiques of population policies' (Silliman 1999: 150). Others felt much more positively about the opportunities offered by the new alliances: 'Feminists are putting pressure on population and family planning agencies to acknowledge women's self-defined needs and our conceptions of reproductive and sexual rights. This should move us closer to social and policy changes that empower women' (Correa and Petchesky 1994:120).

Even if the success of these initiatives was partial, collaboration did lead to considerable progress in the area of reproductive health and rights. What worked were forms of collaboration and solidarity based on mutual understanding among organisations with shared objectives and similar degrees of power. The problems emerged when such relationships linked organisations with unequal power and different ideological positions. The key lesson from the women's movement is the importance of reaching clarity and consensus on the broad aims and principles of a partnership, and avoiding short-term collaborations established solely for the purpose of fund raising, isolated projects, and technocratic interventions.

Girls' education: partnerships in practice

An abundant literature currently reflects on the theories, strategies, and practices of girls' education. It covers such questions as gender gaps in formal education, problems in quality as well as in curriculum reforms, teacher training, and non-formal education (Hulton and Furlong 2001). There is also recognition of the role that 'partnership' plays in education. For example, the Dakar Framework for Action explicitly states that: 'Implementation of the…goals and strategies will…include representatives of all stakeholders and partners and they will operate in transparent and accountable ways' (2000:10).

The UN Girls' Education Initiative (UNGEI), a multi-agency initiative, was announced at the World Education Forum in Dakar by the UN Secretary General Kofi Annan, as a ten-year global programme with the overall objective of demonstrably narrowing the gender gap in primary and secondary education by 2005 and contributing to the achievement of gender equality and universal primary completion by 2015, through action at national, sub-national, and community levels (UNICEF 2002). The initiative was intended to be an open partnership of the United Nations system, governments, donor countries, NGOs, the private sector, and communities and families, in order to make an effective response to issues of poverty, the school environment, and quality of education, as well as adverse cultural practices. Initially, UNGEI harnessed the strengths of 13 different multilateral organisations, by developing a variety of flexible partnerships among themselves and with civil-society institutions.

While the international commitment to partnership for girls' education appears genuine, lack of funds and human resources, lack of clarity about concepts, respective roles, and responsibilities, and about whether engagement should be strongest at the national or at the regional level, all seem to have plagued this promising activity. For example, in the East Asia region, UNESCO attempted to lead the UNGEI initiative. It designed a comprehensive plan of activities, including advocacy and networking, in order to campaign for improvements to the quality and availability of girls' education in countries in the region. However, despite many attempts, only a few UN agencies and other international NGOs became involved – and even those in a limited manner.

UNICEF, entrusted with the task of leading the initiative, has recognised that it had not been providing 'the type of decisive and visionary leadership that was expected from its mandate given in Dakar' (UNICEF 2003). More recently, UNICEF has attempted to revive the initiative through various steps, including the formation of a multi-stakeholder Global Advisory Committee, a focus on the 25 countries most at risk of not meeting the 2005 Goal, instituting a major new information campaign, and linking more energetically to the Fast Track Initiative (FTI). The latter commitment is essential, because the proliferation of 'initiatives' can create structural confusions in partnerships. The importance of a link to the FTI is crucial, because making partnerships operational requires an investment of time and resources, a failure of which can prevent commitments from being translated into practice.

While UNGEI is the largest and perhaps most prestigious partnership for girls' education, contributors to this book demonstrate that many agencies, organisations, and individuals are forging other alliances, with the express purpose of promoting gender equality in education.

The contents of the book

We have attempted to illustrate different kinds of partnership. We break down the universal notion of 'partnership' in the sphere of girls' and women's education into its many different colours and levels, from the global and regional to the national and local. The choice of countries and experiences is a result of a desire to include a variety of geographical experiences, and of organisations diverse in size, reach, and scope. The collection is also an outcome of personal connections with individuals and organisations. It does not claim to be comprehensive in terms of either empirical illustrations or theoretical observations. Another limitation is the fact that the challenges and problems inherent in the partnerships analysed are not always fully exposed. Partly this is due to the fact that many of the relevant initiatives are either new or on-going, and partly to the fact that authors have invested a great deal in them: pride in achievements and a protective attitude sometimes militate against the total exposure of difficulties and weaknesses. Thus problems identified often appear to lie with 'the other' in the partnership, whether this is a government, a donor, an NGO, or a community.

This book consists of three sections.

Prestige and profile

Part One, 'Prestige and Profile', contains chapters illustrating the fact that partnerships enjoying a high profile in terms of the status of their members or their reach are more likely to endure. This is because they have better access to resources, financial and human, that are essential for servicing and maintaining partnerships. Their very nature makes such partnerships both more credible and more visible.

In this section we include three chapters. In the first, on the **Global Campaign for Education (GCE)**, Patrick Watt documents the innovative use of tactics that were more confrontational than any used previously in the field of education reform. More importantly, the breadth of the coalition spans well beyond development and education organisations, to embrace trade unions and campaigners for child rights. In doing so, it crosses the boundaries of power, influence, and financial dependency that often separate Northern from Southern organisations, and grassroots groups from those dedicated to lobbying and policy influencing.

While the uniqueness of the GCE lies in the fact that its members are exclusively civil-society organisations operating at a global level, the defining characteristic of the **Partnership on Sustainable Strategies for Girls' Education**, described by Adaeze Igboemeka, is that its members are multilateral and bilateral institutions. Since this chapter was written, most of the partnership's functions have been transferred to UNGEI and to the 'Beyond Access Project: Gender, Education, and Development', which is a collaboration between the UK government, the Institute of Education at the University of London, and Oxfam GB. Its successes were a result of the influence exercised by the network on other international agencies and national governments. Despite the resources that the partnership enjoyed, it was also faced with challenges, a major one being the fact that members each had their different agendas and systems, which needed to be negotiated thoroughly for agreement to be reached – a fact which detracted from the flexibility to which the partnership aspired.

The chapter about the **Forum for African Women Educationalists (FAWE)** by Penina Mlama describes a network of highly influential female decision makers and educationalists from African countries who realised the importance of political commitment to achieving gender equality in education. The main focus of FAWE has been on influencing policy formulation and effective implementation through public awareness and advocacy, and demonstrating and developing quality provision through its Centres of Excellence.

Discourse and practice

The second section of the book, 'Discourse and Practice', examines some of the tensions that emerge from the first part. It considers the details of the daily functioning of partnerships: from the recognition that each partner has its own roles, capacities, and responsibilities, which form its 'comparative advantage', to the need to allow shifts in these roles and responsibilities. The first chapter, concerning the **Education For All process in the Philippines**, contributed by Rene R. Raya and Raquel dG. Castillo, clearly demonstrates that the government still perceives education as its exclusive business, even though the discourse of partnership has been accepted. The civil-society network, E-net, has been more successful in accommodating the views and approaches of a variety of NGOs than in negotiating a working relationship with the government.

The second chapter in this section, on **partnerships for education in Bangladesh**, by Ahmadullah Mia, argues that the leadership provided by the Prime Minister contributed in no small measure to progress towards gender equality in education over the last decade, and helped to build alliances for a 'national cause'. The author acknowledges the presence of unequal power relations, with government firmly in control of decision making. In this context, civil society has developed strategies to gradually increase its space and influence through networking, research, and public campaigns.

Sheila Aikman's chapter on the **education of indigenous girls in Peru** notes that while in theory 'partnership' reflects a shift from thinking of poor communities and individuals as 'beneficiaries' to casting them in the role of 'stakeholders', the actual practice is much more complex. FENAMED – the Federation of Natives of Madre de Dios – encounters considerable obstacles as it enters into partnerships to compensate for the lack of educated indigenous professionals. It has to interact with 'external agents' who have very different educational aspirations and perceptions of what is relevant and good-quality education. Through the story of 'Magda', the author reflects on how the profoundly gender-segregated and gender-biased reality of much of the Latin American context leads to particularly negative outcomes for indigenous girls.

Scaling up and sustainability

The final part of the book is entitled 'Scaling Up and Sustainability'. Given the magnitude of the task associated with achieving the MDGs for education, it is argued that small initiatives, however innovative and successful, are not enough. Scaling up is essential, as is the embedding of these experiences in long-term, mainstream initiatives. The case study of **community schools in Egypt**, contributed by Malak Zaalouk, reflects on an initially small-scale initiative, mediated through UNICEF. The involvement of the government, and of key stakeholders such as USAID, the World Bank, and the European Union, allowed the scope of the initial idea to be greatly enlarged. The Egyptian experience offers further important lessons: in order to succeed, a partnership requires constant and vigilant political commitment and leadership, appropriate structures, and funding.

The second and final chapter in this section, by Lucy Lake and Angeline Mugwendere, describes the work of **CAMFED (Campaign for Female Education) in sub-Saharan Africa** and its pioneering approach, which places girls and their needs at the centre of education planning and provision. CAMFED's main activity has been to establish links between communities across Africa, creating alliances to mobilise resources, and building local confidence and skills to maintain a 'virtuous circle' that will ensure a smooth transition for girls from primary education to a productive adulthood. The authors maintain that sustainability and the possibility for replication and scaling up are in-built in the model.

By documenting and analysing some of the complexities, challenges, and promises inherent in building partnerships for girls' education, we hope that this book will provide insights into possible strategies for progress, especially towards the achievement of the Millennium Development Goals.

Nitya Rao is a lecturer in Gender and Development at the School of Development Studies, University of East Anglia, England. She has worked extensively in the field of gender analysis and social development, focusing on women's organisation, literacy, and livelihoods for nearly two decades, both as a practitioner and trainer at the grassroots level in India and as a researcher and policy advocate in South Asia and globally.

Ines Smyth is currently a Gender Adviser in Oxfam GB, based in Oxford, England, where she has occupied several posts. Previously she was a lecturer and researcher in a number of academic institutions, including the Institute of Social Studies in the Hague, the University of Oxford, and the Development Studies Institute at the London School of Economics.

Notes

1   This is primarily with reference to the post-colonial, non-socialist states of Asia (particularly South Asia), Africa, and Latin America.

2   While acknowledging the complexity of the debates on the nature of the civil society, in this chapter NGOs, civil-society organisations (CSOs), and community-based organisations (CBOs), though different among themselves, are all included under the term 'civil society'. It should be noted that these terms are often used interchangeably in this book.

3   Korten (1990) identifies these as stages, or what he calls 'generations' in the evolution of NGOs. So for instance, first-generation NGOs did/do focus on relief and welfare, directly delivering services or providing humanitarian assistance in the event of war, natural disasters, and so on. The second-generation NGOs emphasise the self-reliance of local communities. The third generation have turned towards creating an institutional and policy environment which will facilitate and sustain local development action. The fourth generation of NGOs have been pushing for an alternative, people-centred vision of development on a global scale.

4   'Briefly summarised, a SWAp is supposed to provide an integrated programme, setting out policy objectives, a comprehensive policy framework, a detailed investment plan, specific expenditure plans, and detailed funding commitments for government and donors' (Kevin Watkins: *The Oxfam Education Report*, Oxford: Oxfam GB, 2000).

5   Which stemmed from the 1995 Beijing Women's Conference and re-emphasised the Cairo agenda in relation to women's health.

References

Constantino-David, K. (1992) 'The Philippine experience in scaling-up', in Edwards and Hulme (eds.) 1992.

Correa, S. and R. Petchesky (1994) 'Reproductive and sexual rights: a feminist perspective' in G. Sen, A. Germaine, and L. Chen (eds.) *Population Policies Reconsidered: Health, Empowerment and Rights*, Boston, Harvard Series on Population and International Health, Boston MA: Harvard University Press.

Dakar Framework for Action (2000) World Education Forum, Dakar, Senegal.

Dixon-Mueller, R. (1993) *Population Policies and Women's Rights: Transforming Reproductive Choice*, Westport, CT: Praeger.

Edwards, M. (2000) *Future Positive: International Cooperation in the 21st Century*, London: Earthscan.

Edwards, M. and D. Hulme (1992) 'Scaling-up the developmental impact of NGOs: concepts and experiences' in Edwards and Hulme (eds.) 1992.

Edwards, M. and D. Hulme (eds.) (1992) *Making a Difference: NGOs and Development in a Changing World,* London: Save the Children and Earthscan.

Edwards, M., D. Hulme, and T. Wallace (2000) 'Increasing leverage for development: challenges for NGOs in a global future' in Lewis and Wallace (eds.) 2000.

Elu, J. and K. Banya (1999) 'Non-governmental organisations as partners in Africa: a cultural analysis of North-South relations' in L. King and L. Buchert (eds.) *Changing International Aid to Education: Global Patterns and National Contexts,* Paris: UNESCO Publishing.

Fine, B. (1999) 'The development state is dead: long live social capital?', *Development and Change* 30 (1): 1-19.

Fowler, A. (1998) 'Non-governmental Organisations in Africa: Achieving Comparative Advantage in Relief and Micro-development', Institute of Development Studies Discussion Paper 249, Brighton: University of Sussex.

Fowler, A. (2000a) 'Civil Society, NGDO's and Social Development: Changing the Rules of the Game', UNRISD Occasional Paper 1, Geneva: UNRISD.

Fowler, A. (2000b) 'Introduction – beyond partnership: getting real about NGO relationships in the aid system', *IDS Bulletin,* 31(3): 1-13.

Hall, A. (1992) 'From victims to victors: NGOs and empowerment in Itaparica', in Edwards and Hulme (eds.) 1992.

Harriss, J. (2000) *Depoliticising Development: The World Bank and Social Capital,* New Delhi: Leftword Books.

Helmich, H. (1999) 'Introduction' in I. Smillie and H. Helmich (eds.) *Stakeholders: Government–NGO Partnerships for International Development,* London: Earthscan.

Heward, C. (1999) 'Introduction' in C. Heward and S. Bunwaree (eds.) *Gender, Education and Development: Beyond Access to Empowerment,* London: Zed Books.

Holzner, B., N. Kollmann, and S. Darwisyah (2002) *East–West Encounters on Reproductive Health Practices and Policies,* Aksant

Howell, J. and J. Pearce (2000) 'Civil society: technical instrument or social force for change?' in Lewis and Wallace (eds.) 2000.

Hulme, D. and M. Edwards (eds.) (1997) *NGOs, States and Donors: Too Close for Comfort?,* London: Macmillan and the Save the Children Fund.

Hulton, L. and D. Furlong (2001) *Gender Equality in Education: A Select Annotated Bibliography,* Brighton, Sussex: BRIDGE, Institute of Development Studies.

Hyde, K. and S. Miske (2001) *Thematic Studies: Girls' Education,* Paris: UNESCO.

King, K. (1999) 'Introduction: new challenges to international development cooperation in education', in K. King and L. Buchert (eds.) *Changing International Aid to Education: Global Patterns and National Contexts,* Paris: UNESCO Publishing.

Korten, D. (1990) *Getting to the 21st Century: Voluntary Action and the Global Agenda,* West Hartford, CT: Kumarian.

Lewis, D. and T. Wallace (eds.) (2000) *New Roles and Relevance: Development NGOs and the Challenge of Change*, West Hartford, CT: Kumarian.

Mackintosh, M. (1992) 'Questioning the State' in M. Wuytz, M. Mackintosh, T. Hewitt (eds.) *Development Policy and Public Action*, Oxford: Oxford University Press and Open University.

Prakash, S. and P. Selle (eds.) (2004) *Investigating Social Capital: Comparative Perspectives on Civil Society, Participation and Governance*, New Delhi: Sage.

Rose, P. (2003) 'Tracking Progress of the Fast Track Initiative: A Review of the FTI and Indicative Framework for Education Reform', Report prepared for Actionaid on behalf of the Global Campaign for Education, Sussex: Centre for International Education.

Silliman, J. 1999, 'Expanding civil society, shrinking political spaces: the case of women's non-governmental organizations' in J. Silliman and Y. King (eds.) *Dangerous Intersections: Feminism, Population and The Environment*, London and New York: Zed Books.

Subrahmanian, R. (2004) 'The Politics of Resourcing Education: A Review of New Aid Modalities from a Gender Perspective', first draft of paper presented at the Beyond Access Seminar Series, 28 April 2004, Oxford.

Tomasevski, K. (2003) *Education Denied: Costs and Remedies*, London: Zed Books.

Tremayne, S. (2001) 'Introduction' in S. Tremayne (ed.) *Managing Reproductive Life: Cross-Cultural Themes in Fertility and Sexuality*, Oxford: Berghahn Books.

UNDP (2004) *Millennium Project*, Task Force on Education and Gender Equality, New York: UNDP.

UNESCO (2002) *EFA Global Monitoring Report 2002: Is the World on Track?*, The EFA Global Monitoring Report Team, Paris: UNESCO Publishing.

UNESCO (2003) *EFA Global Monitoring Report 2003: Gender and Education For All: The Leap to Equality,* The EFA Global Monitoring Report Team, Paris: UNESCO Publishing.

UNICEF (2002) 'A Concept Note', New York: UNICEF.

UNICEF (2003) 'Information note on recent developments in efforts to accelerate progress on girls' education', email communication from UNICEF, New York.

WEDO (1998) *Mapping Progress: Assessing Implementation of the Beijing Platform of Action,* New York: WEDO.

World Bank (1994) *A New Agenda for Women's Health and Nutrition*, Washington DC: World Bank.

World Bank (1997) *World Development Report 1997: The State in a Changing World,* Washington DC: World Bank.

World Bank (1998) *Assessing Aid: What Works, What Doesn't and Why*, Washington DC: World Bank.

World Bank (2000) *World Development Report 1999/2000: Entering the 21st Century*, Oxford: Oxford University Press.

World Bank (2002) *World Development Report 2002: Building Institutions for Markets*, Oxford: Oxford University Press.

Part One

Prestige and Profile

1 Keeping education on the international agenda: the Global Campaign for Education

Patrick Watt

The Global Campaign for Education was created in 1999 by four international civil-society organisations: Oxfam International, ActionAid, Education International, and the Global March Against Child Labour. At the time, each of them was launching its own advocacy campaign to improve access to education in developing countries.

Oxfam International, a confederation of development NGOs with an extensive track record of high-profile policy-influencing work, but limited experience in the education sector, launched its 'Education Now' campaign early in 1999 with a major report which highlighted the lack of progress towards the goals agreed at the World Conference on Education For All (EFA), held in Jomtien, Thailand, in 1990. At that conference, more than 150 governments had promised that by the year 2000 adult illiteracy rates would be halved, and all children would enjoy the right to a good primary education. Oxfam's report called for a global financing plan to support a renewed international effort to achieve the goals of EFA. The World Bank and UNICEF gave early support to this proposal. Oxfam linked its education campaign closely to its advocacy work aiming to relieve the burden of unsustainable debt in developing countries, and also to its work on aid policy and poverty reduction.

At the same time, ActionAid, a UK-based INGO, began its own education campaign, called 'Elimu' (a Swahili word which means 'Education is Life'). Elimu focused on the establishment of national advocacy networks in developing countries, with the capacity to hold governments to account for their commitments to fund basic education. Meanwhile, Education International (EI) – a global coalition of teachers' unions – decided to focus its advocacy efforts on improving the status of teachers in developing-country education systems. In early 1999, Oxfam, ActionAid, and EI agreed to maximise the impact of their advocacy by collaborating to respond to key international influencing opportunities, especially at the World Education Forum in Dakar in 2000, and by adopting a number of joint 'headline' policy positions and objectives.

Out of these initial discussions, a decision was taken to establish a new 'global campaign for education', which would mobilise a broad constituency of civil-society organisations (CSOs) to press for the elimination of gender disparities in education by the year 2005 and the achievement of universal primary education by the year 2015. The three organisations planned to produce a brief 'mission statement' and agree a set of common actions, a membership structure, and communications plans. Although the plans for a global campaign were initially focused on campaigning at the Dakar forum, they were also developed with a view to creating a broad civil-society 'movement' for the longer term: a movement over which the founder members would have no direct control – similar to the model of the Jubilee debt campaign.

In order to deliver on these plans, two part-time staff based in Novib (Oxfam Netherlands) and Education International worked on a campaign framework with a steering group, consisting of staff in Oxfam, ActionAid, and EI, together with four southern NGOs – the Delhi-based Global March Against Child Labour, and national networks from Bangladesh, Brazil, and South Africa. The Global Campaign for Education (GCE) was formally launched at a meeting of these CSOs in October 1999, with the aim of expanding membership to other CSOs over the coming months. The GCE members agreed to work together initially on two major campaign activities. The first was a 'Global Week of Action' in April 2000, to raise public awareness and support for the objectives of Education For All. The initiatives included press conferences with heads of government and finance ministers, actions by GCE members – such as mailing politicians, urging them to support a global financing plan prior to the summit meeting in Dakar – and intensive media work in the UK, the USA, the Netherlands, and elsewhere. In addition to the 'Week of Action', other activities were planned in the weeks leading up to the forum in Dakar, including writing letters to political leaders, organising seminars and conferences, and lobbying government ministers and officials. The GCE also established a website, compiled an electronic list for civil-society activists, and wrote a joint proposal, 'A Compact for Africa', which called for a concerted multilateral effort to achieve the EFA goals in the region.

The second set of major activities took place around the Dakar summit itself, later in the same month. At Dakar, several hundred NGO participants attended a preparatory conference, organised by the UNESCO Collective Consultation on NGOs in EFA and Literacy (CCNGO). Although NGOs failed in their efforts to win additional space for civil-society participation in the official meeting, some members of international NGOs (INGOs) were invited to join national delegations – that of the UK was one example – and in the course of the summit the GCE became largely accepted as a legitimate umbrella body for civil-society participants. Daily briefings, targeted lobbying of national delegations, participation in drafting the EFA framework for action, and media work ensured that the GCE had a highly visible presence at the summit, and helped to establish a new space for advocacy on education.

A new kind of civil-society partnership in education

The GCE marked a significant departure from previous civil-society advocacy work on education, which until then had mainly employed an 'insider' strategy of engaging in technical and professional discussion behind closed doors. Unlike debates on improvements in health care, water supply, or agriculture, debates on the development of education services were largely invisible to people outside the sector. Most of the civil-society groups involved in these discussions were either specialised practitioners working in complementary niches alongside government (for example, non-formal education organisations), or professional groups (for example, consultancy agencies reliant on donor-funded technical assistance). Now a new dimension was added by the use of more confrontational tactics and tightly focused, media-friendly messages, from development organisations with a track record of public campaigning. By using advocacy briefings, targeted lobbying, and press releases to publicise the lack of progress on education reform, and by challenging existing ways of working, the GCE created tensions at Dakar. Many education specialists in governments and donor agencies were unused to being lobbied so directly, and in some cases they sought to defend their professional boundaries by questioning the expertise and legitimacy of GCE members.[1] For some civil-society groups in the CCNGO – UNESCO's forum for consultation with NGOs on education – the GCE's approach was seen as unduly critical (especially of UNESCO, with which many CCNGO members had a close working relationship) and as a threat to a broad professional consensus about how best to achieve Education For All. (See, for example, UNESCO 2000.)

The GCE was distinctive for more than its advocacy style. Unlike the CCNGO, which before 2001 included few Southern civil-society organisations, the GCE was explicitly intended as an alliance of Northern *and* Southern civil society, which combined advocacy experience and lobby access to Northern decision-makers with national-level policy knowledge and grassroots programme experience. This helped to root Northern INGO advocacy in the realities of poor people's lives in the South, while giving Southern NGOs access to information and influencing opportunities which had previously been denied to them. So campaigning for free basic education by Oxfam and ActionAid was based on joint research and advocacy with national and local civil-society organisations in the South, while Southern NGOs were given a platform in Washington DC to argue the case for free education to a sceptical audience of World Bank and USAID staff.[2]

The GCE was also distinctive for the breadth of the coalition, which extended beyond NGOs working on education and international development to include other civil-society organisations, such as trade unions and campaigners against child labour – organisations which have both a distinctive perspective on education policy, and the capacity to mobilise large numbers of supporters, thereby making the GCE (indirectly) a mass-membership organisation. This potential of this membership base for mass actions began to be realised with the planning of 'The World's Biggest Lesson' in April 2003.

Finally, the GCE was distinctive for the closeness of the collaboration between its members. Other national and international education alliances and networks had tended to function as forums for policy discussion, confining themselves to communication rather than co-ordination. Joint lobbying on shared policy positions, and the pooling of resources that took place during and after Dakar, represented a major step forwards in terms of civil-society coalition building. In addition to the practical benefits of close joint work, it gave greater resonance and legitimacy to the GCE's appeal to donors and governments to enter into – and act upon – a global compact for education. Civil-society organisations were leading by example, by sacrificing some pride and prejudice for the sake of achieving together what they could not achieve individually.

Despite the tensions created by the GCE's emergence as a major civil-society voice on education, the stark failure of the international community during the 1990s to deliver on the commitments made at Jomtien meant that the GCE's messages resonated with many participants at Dakar, including members of official delegations – as evinced by public endorsements of the GCE from the UN Secretary General and the heads of the World Bank, UNDP, UNICEF, and UNESCO, and the extent to which key GCE demands were reflected in the Dakar Framework for Action (Murphy and Mundy 2002).

Securing high-profile support for the campaign and pushing education up the agenda of the international community were two obvious early achievements on the part of the GCE. Yet in the wake of the Dakar summit, the international community delivered on very few of the commitments made in the Framework for Action. Progress was stalled by disagreements among governments and donors over what would be entailed by 'national EFA plans', how they fitted within pre-existing sectoral planning processes and poverty-reduction strategies, and which organisation should have overall responsibility for the process. There was a failure to agree on the content or scope of a 'Global Initiative' for education, designed to deliver on the pledge that 'no country seriously committed to Education For All will be thwarted in their achievement of this goal by a lack of resources'. In particular, donors were reluctant both to commit significant additional resources to education and to cede a leading role to UNESCO, which many of them regarded as lacking in both capacity and credibility.

After the Dakar summit, the GCE's lobbying and campaigning activity initially subsided, and the interest and commitment of political leaders and media waned. However, in early 2001 GCE members resolved to re-ignite the campaign – once it became clear that little or no movement was taking place among donors and governments to meet key commitments. The following actions were taken.

- A GCE proposal for a Global Initiative for Education was agreed among members, and the text was disseminated in English and French.

- Lobby meetings were held with key donor agencies, including the World Bank, UNICEF, UNESCO, and government ministries of the UK, Netherlands, and Canada, in an effort to secure a commitment to develop a multilateral planning, finance, and monitoring initiative to achieve the EFA goals.

- The Board of the World Bank was pressed to deliver real, measurable progress on education, and to take a more proactive role in mobilising commitments by governments and donors, in concert with the UN agencies.

- Renewed media activity was stimulated by the involvement of high-profile campaign supporters – such as Nelson Mandela and the UK and Canadian Finance Ministers, Gordon Brown and Paul Martin – who made public statements calling for progress on access to education.

Such efforts helped to bring together the 'like-minded' donor group (World Bank, UNICEF, UNESCO, Netherlands, Norway, Canada, EC, UK, and occasionally others) in late 2001 to develop plans for a new multi-donor initiative. The World Bank undertook detailed background analytical work to argue the case for such an initiative and suggest how it could be developed. Out of these discussions, a 'Fast Track Initiative' (FTI) for education was launched at the IMF–World Bank meetings in April 2002. While the FTI is at an early stage in its implementation, and inadequate donor funding is a major obstacle to progress, the initiative nonetheless contains important elements of the 'global compact' for education to which donors and developing-country governments committed themselves at Dakar. (See, for example, ActionAid 2003.)

Institutionalising the GCE

At about the same time, the GCE members decided to institutionalise the campaign. Before and during the Dakar summit, GCE positions had been developed in a largely *ad hoc* way, and there was little central co-ordinating capacity for the campaign. In part this was because, when the GCE was initially launched, the time leading up to Dakar was seen as something of a 'trial period' for a previously untested campaigning approach, and there was no definite plan to extend its lifespan beyond the summit. Yet the early advocacy successes achieved at Dakar, and strong demand from other civil-society organisations to join the campaign, made a strong case for the GCE's work to be put on a more permanent basis.

As a result, campaign members meeting in Delhi in February 2001 agreed a structure for the coalition, with the aim of creating a member-driven organisation, able to develop a strategic programme of work and increase its public profile. The following changes in the 18 months after the Delhi meeting helped to institutionalise the GCE.

- A mission statement, which aspiring members must sign, was agreed; and a fee-based membership structure was established.

- A board structure was established. GCE members elect a 12-person board every two years, drawn from its membership organisations, at a biennial meeting. The board – which meets on a regular basis and is accountable to members – guides the development of campaign strategy, manages the budget, and oversees the work of a small secretariat. It is designed to be broadly representative of GCE's membership, with a majority of board members drawn from Southern civil-society organisations. GCE members can propose actions and positions to the board, usually through the secretariat.

- A secretariat was established, initially based in the EI offices in Brussels. At present there are two staff, one of whom works as a full-time advocacy co-ordinator. The secretariat co-ordinates advocacy and campaign activities among members, provides regular newsletter updates to members, and works to increase the GCE's profile (for example, by enlisting high-profile supporters) and extend its membership base.

- A GCE website and logo were established.

- The GCE was legally constituted, with its own separate bank account.

As the coalition acquired a firmer institutional footing, it branched out into new advocacy work, gaining profile and new members. During 2001 and 2002, GCE members did intensive advocacy and campaign work on education financing, taking advantage of various international processes associated with the UN's Financing for Development summit in Monterrey, IMF–World Bank meetings, and meetings of the G8, the United Nations General Assembly, the World Summit on Sustainable Development, the UN Girls' Education Initiative (UNGEI), and other opportunities. Increasingly, GCE members were uniting under the GCE banner: letters and regular policy briefings for international lobbying carried the GCE logo, despite having usually been written by staff of member organisations. More significantly, the policy positions in these papers were being negotiated and agreed among GCE members, through the board. In international meetings where civil society was given seats, the GCE began to operate as a coherent group, developing lobby strategies in advance – for example, at the first meeting of the UNESCO High Level Group in Paris in late 2001, where two places in the communiqué drafting group were allocated to the GCE. In a number of countries, including the USA and the UK, and in Brussels, local staff of GCE member organisations worked closely together on lobbying and research – for example, by regularly meeting with their governments as a bloc.

New members, representing civil society at international, regional, and national levels, joined the campaign after early 2001. Some of them were specialist education organisations, and others were working on broader issues of development, human rights, and social justice. These new members – including World Vision, Public Services International, Forum for African Women Educationalists (FAWE), Save the Children Alliance, Asian South Pacific Bureau of Adult Education (ASBPAE), Consejo de Educación de Adultos de America Latina (CEAAL: Latin America Adult Education Council), VSO (Voluntary Service Overseas), Fe y Alegría, and Ibis – added new dimensions to the work of the GCE. For example, the growing number of European NGOs in the campaign made it possible in April 2003 for the GCE to co-ordinate EU-wide lobbying of member-state governments, members of the European Parliament, and the European Commission for increased aid to education, as part of the Global Week of Action. Similarly, the GCE secretariat worked closely with African civil-society groups – themselves organised in a regional network, ANCEFA – that were doing joint advocacy work with national governments at the conference of Ministers of African Education (MINEDAF) in Dar es Salaam in November 2002.

The GCE has also actively encouraged the creation of national advocacy coalitions. Many of these coalitions – bringing together NGOs, community groups, unions, religious organisations, academics, and other stakeholders – were created at the time of the Dakar summit, in an effort to put citizen pressure on governments to act on their education commitments. About 25 of these coalitions have since become active members of the GCE, representing about 250 groups. In addition to countries where national coalitions exist, GCE members are now active in approximately 80 countries, representing an extra-ordinary range of knowledge and experience. In early 2003, organisations in a total of more than 100 countries around the world participated in the GCE's annual Global Action Week.

The Global Week of Action: putting partnership into practice

The GCE's focal point for collaboration is the Global Week of Action, which has taken place each April since the first one in 2000, and has grown steadily in its scale and impact. During the Week of Action, GCE members organise national-level campaign activities around a common theme and message, while also taking part in a joint international event. For example, in 2002 the Week's theme was the impact of education costs on access to schooling, under the campaign slogan 'Free to Learn'. Member organisations organised protests, publicity stunts, mailings by supporters, fact-finding trips for the media and politicians, conferences, round-table policy debates, opinion features in newspapers, and other initiatives in 90 countries. At the same time, GCE members mobilised their supporters to participate in a global mailing to G8 leaders, calling on them to give their political and financial backing to the Education Fast Track Initiative. This action was supported by GCE lobby meetings with government officials in the run-up to the G8 summit meeting in Kananaskis in 2002, and GCE participation in a civil-society consultation with the G8 education task force. The Week of Action has three purposes:

- it creates wider public awareness of education issues, and the profile of the GCE;

- it puts pressure on governments to deliver on the commitments that they made at Dakar, by demonstrating the presence of a constituency for education;

- and it is a concrete way in which GCE members can work together, developing trust, knowledge, and confidence within the coalition.

Each year, the theme of the Week of Action is negotiated across the coalition. An annual questionnaire is issued to member organisations, asking which theme they want to be addressed. A shortlist is then submitted to the board for a final decision, after which a planning group, consisting of campaign, media, and policy staff from key member organisations, works with the secretariat to develop the strategy, message, and materials for the Week of Action.

A range of options was discussed by the board for the Week of Action in 2003; they included the status of teachers, child labour, adult literacy, and gender disparities in education. Gender and education was selected as the theme, with a focus on the 2005 MDG target of eliminating gender disparities in school enrolments. There were two rationales for choosing gender: first, its immediacy, with the 2005 goal fast approaching and failure unavoidable for a large number of developing countries; and, second, its accessibility and potential for mobilising large numbers of children and adults. The following actions took place during the 2003 Week of Action.

- The world's biggest-ever lesson, drawing attention to inequalities in education, was organised by GCE members, in collaboration with schools in more than 100 countries. The lesson involved almost two million children and adults, attracting widespread media coverage and high-level political support from the UN and national governments.

- A major new GCE research report was published. 'A Fair Chance' identified the steps needed to eliminate gender disparities in education. Based on original research in nine African and Asian countries, it was disseminated to key decision-makers and funded by the UK government's Department for International Development (DFID), the Commonwealth Education Fund, Oxfam, and ActionAid. The research was jointly commissioned by ActionAid, ASPBAE, the Forum for African Women Educationalists (FAWE), and Oxfam.

- Lobby and press work was carried out in association with the IMF–World Bank Spring Meetings, which coincided with the Week of Action, to raise the profile of education in Development Committee discussions. This resulted in stories and messages in the *Washington Post, New York Times, Wall St. Journal*, and BBC World Service Radio.

- Letters were sent from supporters to politicians in several countries, calling on governments to deliver the resources and policy reforms needed to achieve the 2005 goal. In the UK, NGOs and the teachers' unions delivered 60,000 letters to the Chancellor, Gordon Brown.

- National-level protests, stunts, media actions, seminars, and briefings were organised in most countries with an active GCE membership.

- Follow-up lobbying took place in association with the UNGEI and the Girls' Education Partnership – jointly convened by UNICEF, the World Bank, and DFID – with the aim of pushing girls' education higher up the agenda of donor agencies and the international community.

The Week of Action has become an increasingly prominent and effective example of the GCE's partnership principles being put into practice; moreover, it has broadened that partnership by mobilising new sets of supporters, such as teachers and school children. In media terms, it has become sufficiently well known to be able to dispense with a media 'peg' such as a UN summit: GCE actions such as the world's biggest lesson create their own news story. The Week of Action also demonstrates that the GCE has a constituency which goes beyond the INGO policy staff who usually lead lobbying at international meetings; and it has established a popular legitimacy that civil society is sometimes claimed not to have.[3]

Successes

In campaign terms, the GCE has scored significant success in a number of areas. Education has been high up on the political agenda at major international meetings, such as the IMF–World Bank Annual Meetings[4] and at the G8 summit in Kananaskis, Canada, in 2002, where Canada established an education task force to recommend actions to world leaders. While it is difficult to attribute this entirely to the GCE's activities, staff in many donor agencies have remarked upon the importance of the GCE in keeping education on the 'radar screens' of politicians. Modest – but in the current climate significant – increases in aid for education have occurred since the Dakar summit, from donors including Canada, the Netherlands, the USA, and the UK. The GCE has helped to create an environment in which such pledges are important and are seen as politically popular (Murphy and Mundy 2002).

This success can be attributed to a number of factors. First, the GCE has built a sufficiently broad and deep coalition to mobilise large numbers of supporters from both North and South, around a simple and readily understandable set of messages: that *education is a basic right*, and *an achievable right*, and that *governments in both North and South must deliver now on their commitment to achieve EFA*. By relying on the capacity of its members to develop campaigns – rather than appointing a larger GCE secretariat to take the lead – the coalition has been able to secure lobby access and generate political support through its members' existing contacts and relationships. For example, Oxfam's relationships with the economist Amartya Sen and the UN Secretary General's office have been decisive in securing their support for the GCE's messages. Similarly, the research and campaigns capacity of many of the member organisations has been crucial in developing the global Week of Action as a major international campaign activity – to the point where UNESCO has sought to associate its own EFA week with the Week of Action, by holding it at the same time.

The breadth of the GCE and its member-driven, democratic character have given its messages a power and legitimacy that is missing from the campaign of any individual coalition member. Governments are often more receptive to campaign messages coming from a transnational coalition; or at the very least they find it more difficult to dismiss them as the ideas of an unrepresentative and unelected few. At Dakar, and subsequently, donors and governments have for the most part seen the GCE as a legitimate umbrella for civil-society organisations working in education, as reflected in invitations to the GCE to occupy the civil-society seat at various meetings and consultations, including that of the G8 education task force and the World Bank–Netherlands Education For All

Conference in February 2002. The existence of a broad-based coalition such as the GCE also largely relieves governments of the problem of deciding which civil-society organisations they should speak to, and it enables them to communicate to a large cross-section of civil-society organisations quickly and simply, through the secretariat.

At international meetings, in the media, and in discussions among civil-society representatives, the GCE has been instrumental in creating a space for Southern civil society to articulate its needs and priorities. For example, the GCE delegation to the UNESCO High Level Group Meeting in Abuja in November 2002 was led by coalition members from India and Brazil, giving access to developing-country education ministers that would have been difficult had the lobbying been led by Northern INGOs. International initiatives are essential when the GCE is seeking to influence multilateral processes, such as the Education Fast Track Initiative, which has a large number of differing advocacy targets. Being able to undertake a co-ordinated lobby of World Bank–IMF Executive Directors and development ministers at World Bank–IMF meetings, drawing on research material generated by GCE members in the South, is one example of the potential of the GCE for implementing complex international influencing strategies.

Problems and challenges

At the same time, working in coalition generates inevitable tensions and poses challenges. The GCE is a diffuse group, whose members have very different areas of expertise, capacities, and policy priorities. The GCE membership ranges from highly professionalised INGOs with annual budgets in excess of $100m, to small, recently established, and financially insecure national education networks in low-income countries; it embraces popular campaigning groups, teachers' unions, and non-formal education service deliverers. Reaching consensus among these groups can be a complicated process. For example, to what extent should the GCE focus on Universal Primary Education (UPE) as its principal campaign objective? There is an on-going debate within the coalition about this issue – especially among organisations whose expertise is in adult literacy, early childhood development, or non-formal education, who argue that the GCE should promote a more balanced, 'holistic' approach to education development. In contrast, many campaigning organisations argue that it makes tactical sense for the GCE to focus its advocacy efforts on an international goal for which there exists strong political support, and which is readily understandable by a wider public. So far, the campaign has sought to compromise on this question, by devoting significant effort to advocacy associated with the Fast Track Initiative on education, while calling for more balanced education development across the sub-sectors in countries' sector plans. (See, for example, GCE 2002.)

Similarly, there are differences among members on the question of whether the GCE has struck the right balance between international campaigning on finance issues (concentrated in the North, around the international financial institutions, the UN, and donor governments) and campaigning on other education issues which may have more relevance in the South, such as the quality of services, choice of teaching methods, and the status of teachers. These tensions can to some extent be resolved by changing the focus of the Week of Action each year, so that different issues can be given campaign space. They can also be partly addressed by keeping the campaign focus as broad as possible, using 'headline' messages and slogans that can be adapted to local conditions. For example, gender – the focus of the 2003 Week of Action report – was seen as a lower priority for Latin American members of the campaign, in a region where enrolment and completion rates for girls are often higher than for boys. Therefore the campaign materials focused on 'equity in education' rather than gender itself, so that the needs of other disadvantaged groups – such as indigenous populations – could be highlighted.

However, the problem remains that the greatest capacity among members, in terms of resources, personnel, and lobby access, rests in the INGOs and other international organisations that belong to the GCE. Inevitably this fact influences the choice of campaign priorities, even where a Southern-dominated board structure exists. Some of the obstacles to greater involvement of Southern civil society are practical: working in coalition is generally more difficult in the South, where telecommunications and transport links are often inefficient and expensive, and where there is often only a small pool of skilled and experienced CSO staff. The GCE's lobby agenda for international meetings tends to be set mainly by Northern-based members who are able to communicate swiftly and at short notice, whose first language is English, and who are familiar with the institutions that the campaign is seeking to influence. Other obstacles arise from lack of knowledge and self-confidence, and the fact that certain sorts of knowledge are valued above others in international advocacy campaigns. Although the Southern-based GCE members have extensive knowledge of grassroots education work and understand the policy environment in their own countries, often this knowledge has not been well integrated into the lobby work done by NGOs at international decision-making meetings – at least partly because it is not always a priority for INGOs. Moreover, the sorts of knowledge that Southern civil society possesses are often not the sort of knowledge that will influence policy in international institutions like the World Bank, where an understanding of finance issues and donor policy – of which the INGOs have greater experience – may be more important in enabling civil society to engage in debates.

Related to this, the unequal levels of funding and influence within civil society mirror the more general political and economic asymmetries between North and South. For example, most international decision-making meetings take place in the North, and have their agendas set by Northern-based international organisations and bilateral donor agencies. This tends to exclude Southern civil society still further and distort campaign priorities. It is often difficult for Southern civil-society representatives to obtain the cash, visas, and accreditation needed to attend international meetings, especially at short notice. Once there, Southern civil-society staff often encounter debates that are dominated by the donor agencies and seem far removed from the priorities in their own countries.

These disparities in capacity between Northern and Southern civil society cannot be easily resolved, however enthusiastically the GCE promotes a model of partnership. This is especially so where Southern networks and coalitions remain heavily dependent, as is currently the case, on funding and support from civil society in the North. At the same time, moves within the GCE to relocate its secretariat to the South, diversify the funding base, and build the independent advocacy capacity of Southern civil society are starting to address these urgent issues.

Tensions exist within the coalition regarding the nature of the GCE's relation-ship with international institutions and governments, and the extent to which 'insider' tactics of private lobbying should be used, rather than more public, 'outsider' tactics involving confrontational campaigning. Although in practice the GCE has employed both approaches at different points, the two cannot easily be used simultaneously without jeopardising lobby relationships with key decision makers. These relationships have been criticised as too 'cosy' by some GCE members, especially in connection with the World Bank – whose role in education is viewed with deep suspicion by many CSOs, particularly those based in the South. Equally, some GCE members feel that the campaign has failed to be sufficiently critical of UNESCO's role in furthering progress towards the goals of Education For All, but other members maintain a close relationship with UNESCO, through the CCNGO and other forums. For many Southern networks, meanwhile, neither an insider nor an outsider approach to campaigning is straightforward – for example, where government is hostile towards civil society. In such cases, Southern civil-society organisations are often sceptical of the value of advocacy, especially where there is a weak link between public policy and practice, which makes advocacy for change particularly difficult. In such cases, the campaign approach used by the GCE at the international level may be inappropriate, and there may be a need for less public advocacy work in favour of incremental action to secure government commitment to EFA.

Finally, in addition to tensions among members over policy priorities, there is disquiet about some policies and practice that are perceived to be inconsistent across the coalition. For example, some teachers' unions have expressed concerns about NGO funding for non-formal education systems, which in some countries operate in parallel to the public system and are alleged to undermine the collective wage-bargaining power of teachers, by providing lower salary levels and poorer working conditions. Conversely, some NGOs have claimed that unions are obstacles to an expansion of the education system in some countries, where they are devoting their attention to improving the wages and working conditions of existing members, rather than meeting the needs of out-of-school children. While these differences are unlikely to disappear – indeed, their existence often testifies both to the members' commitment to the GCE, and to the coalition's diversity – the board structure and a willingness among members to engage in honest internal discussion have so far ensured that they do not become an insurmountable barrier to joint working.

Where do we go from here?

In the four years of its existence, the GCE has achieved remarkable progress in raising the international profile of education. Although its precise impact on education policy and practice is difficult to gauge, it is likely that the international community's follow-up to the EFA commitments made at the Dakar summit would have been much weaker without the pressure exerted by the campaign. This achievement has been possible because of the partnership-based approach developed through the GCE. Although civil-society organisations have collaborated closely on other issues such as debt relief, the GCE represents a new kind of approach to campaigning on education: linking Northern and Southern civil society, developing shared policy positions and an advocacy strategy, and pooling staff and resources to advance common objectives. This approach has generated significant benefits, in terms of co-ordinated transnational campaigning; more space for Southern civil society to influence advocacy targets; Northern research and advocacy that is better rooted in Southern realities; and the creation of a legitimate and broadly representative umbrella body for CSOs which is able to enter into a constructive dialogue with governments and donors. At the same time, working in such a diverse coalition on a complex range of issues and campaign targets generates inevitable tensions among members – especially where capacities, expertise, and policy priorities differ. Nonetheless, the board structure and a culture of open debate within the GCE have so far prevented these tensions from limiting the GCE's effectiveness.

The key question now facing the GCE is *'Where do we go from here?'* As the partnership seeks to build on the success of recent global Weeks of Action, to broaden its membership base further (especially in regions where it is currently less active, such as North America, the Middle East, East Asia, and the transition countries), and to develop the capacity of Southern members to initiate and lead campaign actions within the coalition, a discussion is taking place about how best to make this all happen. Moving the secretariat to the South in 2005 will help to shift the centre of gravity of the campaign, while the secretariat itself is likely to be expanded, to give it greater capacity to engage with national education networks and support regional advocacy activities – such as those carried out by the African NGO education network, ANCEFA. At the same time, the GCE is working to diversify its funding base, making it less dependent on the small number of INGOs and international organisations that provide the majority of its financial and practical support. In time, this should reduce the disproportionate influence of the campaign's founders over the direction of the coalition, thereby helping to achieve a better balance between the needs and priorities of all members. Finally, the success of the 2003 Week of Action, which involved approximately two million children, young people, and teachers around the world, has mobilised a major new constituency for the GCE and opened up promising opportunities for mass campaigning. By seizing these opportunities, consolidating the campaign, and continuing to work to put the principles of partnership into practice, the GCE can make a crucial contribution to achieving the international education goals adopted at Dakar.

Patrick Watt is a Senior Policy Adviser at ActionAid UK, having previously worked on education issues for both Oxfam and the World Bank. He has done extensive research and lobbying on behalf of the Global Campaign, with particular reference to the World Bank Fast Track Initiative. He has written widely on gender and education, and jointly co-ordinated 'A Fair Chance', the GCE report on the 2005 gender and education target.

Notes

1   For example, a letter from Dieter Berstecher at UNESCO to Kevin Watkins at Oxfam GB, in early 2001, questioned Oxfam's long-term commitment to education and attacked the campaign message as simplistic. Similar comments about the campaign objectives were made by Clare Short, former UK International Development Secretary, in letters to the GCE.

2   Seminar at the Brookings Institution, Washington, DC, March 2002.

3   See for example the 'NGO Watch' project, established by two corporate-funded US think-tanks, the American Enterprise Institute and the Federalist Society. www.ngowatch.org

4   In November 2002, at the postponed Annual Meetings, the World Bank Development Committee discussed education as a main agenda item for the first time in its history.

References

ActionAid (2001) 'Preliminary Review of the Elimu Campaign', London: ActionAid.

ActionAid (2003) 'Fast Track or Back Track?', London: ActionAid.

GCE (2001) 'World Conference on Education – New Delhi', report.

GCE (2002) 'Broken Promises: Why the donors must deliver on the EFA Education Action Plan', lobby briefing.

GCE (2003) 'Campaign and Lobby Strategy 2003–04', draft.

Murphy, L. and K. Mundy (2002) 'A Review of International Nongovernmental EFA Campaigns'.

Oxfam International (1999) 'Education Now: Break the Cycle of Poverty', campaign strategy paper, Oxford: Oxfam GB.

UNESCO (2000) 'A Reason for Hope: the Support of NGOs to Education For All', CCNGO Assessment, Paris: UNESCO.

2 Flying high: the Partnership on Sustainable Strategies for Girls' Education

Adaeze Igboemeka

This chapter[1] considers some of the strengths of the Partnership on Sustainable Strategies for Girls' Education, which has brought together several international development agencies to co-ordinate their efforts to tackle gender inequality in education. From the point of view of one of the partner agencies,[2] it examines the factors that have made the Partnership successful, some of the challenges that have confronted it, and the strategies employed to address those challenges.

The Partnership on Sustainable Strategies for Girls' Education is a multi-donor partnership, initiated in 1998 with financing from the World Bank, the UK government's Department for International Development (DFID), UNICEF, and the Rockefeller Foundation. Today, the main partners are the World Bank, DFID, and UNICEF. The secretariat is based at the World Bank, where the day-to-day activities and work programme of the Partnership are managed.

The Millennium Development Goals (MDGs) and the Education For All movement provide an agreed international framework for achieving gender equality in education. It is in the context of reaching these targets that the Partnership is pursuing better education opportunities for girls. The Partnership's approach has evolved over time. Initially, from 1999 to 2001 its work focused on evaluating girls' education programmes to draw out and disseminate lessons learned from experience. Since 2002, the Partnership's approach has centred on influencing and informing national policies and programmes, often by first producing analytical work and then bringing together the main stakeholders to examine the evidence and build strategies around it.

So far, the successes of the Partnership have been due to its engagement with international and national initiatives, and its influence within the partner organisations. At these three levels, the Partnership has succeeded in bringing together principal players to work towards a common goal of achieving gender equity in education; opening up a forum for sharing information and for broadening debate and dialogue on girls' education; and adding value by developing strong relationships which have led to a common understanding among the partners on how to tackle gender inequalities in education.

Achievements specific to each level of engagement will be illustrated in this chapter. Working in this way has of course produced challenges, the greatest of which has been maintaining the momentum of activity while honouring the commitment to close collaboration, which has at certain times slowed down progress. Some of these difficulties, and the Partnership's responses to them, are considered below.

Engagement at the international level

The partners originally agreed to engage actively in selected countries, providing technical and financial support for education-sector programme work. More recently, the Partnership has turned its attention to influencing and supporting a number of strategic global initiatives, such as the Fast Track Initiative (FTI). Support for mainstreaming gender-equity policies within the FTI is particularly important, in order to ensure that girls' education is addressed in its country-specific plans. Because the Partnership has established its credibility at the international level, it has received requests from the FTI Secretariat to assess policies on girls' education in country proposals. Assessments have already been completed for several countries, and this work will continue, ensuring that plans are adequately addressing gender inequity before they are implemented.

UNICEF has been mandated to lead and co-ordinate the international community to help to achieve the Millennium Development Goal of eliminating gender disparities in school enrolments by 2005, through the United Nations Girls' Education Initiative (UNGEI). The Partnership has been keen to offer its resources to UNGEI, because this is a very important global initiative which specifically targets girls' education. At the Partnership consultative meeting in May 2003, it was decided that the Partnership would support UNGEI in its work at the country level. Such a link could result in major progress towards meeting the gender-equity targets.[3]

Working at the national level

There has been consensus among the members that the Partnership's broad approach would be to offer technical expertise and an increased knowledge base in order to inform governments' policies and programmes. One of the lessons learned from past large-scale multi-agency initiatives on girls' education was that working independently from government made it difficult to sustain effective changes. Influencing government policy on gender equity in education within Poverty Reduction Strategy Papers (PRSPs)[4] and sector plans, and supporting the effective implementation of policy, will have some of the most sustainable results for girls' education.

So far the Partnership has engaged in Peru, Bolivia, Ecuador, Egypt, Bangladesh, Nigeria, and the Democratic Republic of Congo. Activities have begun in Yemen, where gender disparities in primary education are particularly acute. The Partnership's highest priority is to foster national ownership of action plans. Responding quickly to governments' requests for assistance is seen as essential. As will become evident from some of the examples below, the Partnership works to fill the gaps, either where data are lacking or where funds are unavailable. Working in this way has required the Partnership to be highly flexible and responsive, and to develop the capacity to act quickly. This has been one of the strengths of the Partnership: it is able to move quickly into a country, but at the same time remain responsive and adaptable to that particular country's needs.

Bangladesh

Being adaptable and responsive to varying national contexts is a labour-intensive process, but it is an essential component of gender mainstreaming. A one-size-fits-all approach does not work: flexibility is essential if the Partnership is to respond at the national level to support specific needs. Its recent work in Bangladesh resulted from a direct request for assistance from the government. The Bangladeshi government wanted to assess its well-known girls' scholarship system, in order to gauge its success in targeting recipients. The Partnership undertook social assessments, conducting studies which examined the attitudes to and expectations of education in communities, schools, and households.[5] The results gave considerable insight into gender dynamics and were disseminated in a range of consultative workshops with the government to assist ministers and officials to make policy decisions.[6] In Bangladesh, there are many donors operating in the education sector, but the Partnership was able to move in and fill the gaps identified by the government.

Bolivia

The Partnership's work in Bolivia demonstrates the nature of its earlier evaluation activities. But it also illustrates the catalytic nature of its work. The Bolivian Ministry of Education had been working to assess what progress it had achieved with its education-reform programme. The Partnership financed a review of education policies and programmes, intended to improve educational opportunities for vulnerable groups, particularly girls and indigenous groups. This report and other studies supported by the Partnership have contributed to the education components of Bolivia's PRSP.[7] The analytical work, carried out for the government, was catalytic in that it brought together key players to discuss gender issues, and then successfully fed directly into national education policy. Again, being able to respond quickly and disseminate evidence to key players has been essential to making an impact on policy decisions.

Peru

To undertake this kind of quick, catalytic research requires access to high-quality consultants, both national and international. In Peru, the Partnership supported dialogue between government and civil society on education policy for rural and indigenous girls. The Partnership funded GRADE, a national NGO, to carry out several pieces of analytical work on gender equity and ethnicity in rural areas. This work was then fed into workshops organised by Foro Educativo, the most powerful and vocal civil-society voice on education in Peru. So the Partnership seeks to use the research that it supports as evidence for influencing policy, and as a starting point from which national stakeholders can discuss and debate strategies.

Cross-border initiatives

The Partnership has also provided an opportunity to share information across countries. This has been especially valuable in Latin America, where, in some countries like Bolivia, gender disparities and ethnic-group disparities have decreased, while in others disparities have actually increased. The Partnership has facilitated regional discussions at which the results of research examining reasons for these differences have been disseminated. In October 2002, the Partnership co-financed the Conference on Ethnicity, Race, Gender and Education in Latin America, which provided a venue for sharing lessons with policy makers, researchers, and various organisations from across the region.

Approaches that have been successful for improving gender equity in education can be adapted and adopted in other contexts. This is why the Partnership's website (www.girlseducation.org) has been an important information-sharing resource. Managed by an independent consultant, the website provides research findings, training materials, and information on large-scale education programmes for girls, and offers publications and updates on Partnership activities.

Adding value to the partner institutions

One of the Partnership's defining principles has been a high degree of participation, collaboration, and commitment, not only in the direction and financing of the work, but also on technical and substantive issues. This means that the success and sustainability of the Partnership are highly dependent on the efforts of individuals from the partner agencies. The varying levels of commitment and representation in partner organisations have clearly been a weakness in the Partnership. For example, in 2001, a pause in activities resulted from changes in agency staff which left a gap in Partnership representation.

However, revived impetus came in 2002, with a focus on the gender-equity MDG.[8] The close working relationships that have developed from the Partnership have helped to focus international attention on girls' education. By jointly promoting a common position, the agency representatives are supporting each other to ensure that girls' education is given a higher priority, both among the international community and within their own organisations.

For example, in 2002 the Partnership launched activities in Nigeria in co-ordination with the government's Universal Basic Education programme, which is being financed by the World Bank with considerable technical support from DFID. The Partnership undertook a diagnostic study of girls' education and moved on to conduct participatory social assessments. Workshops were then co-ordinated in seven states, in order to develop state strategies for improving girls' educational opportunities. This work involved close collaboration with UNICEF and DFID representatives in Nigeria. The Action Plans on gender equity that emerged from the workshops will now feed into the government's Interim Poverty Reduction Strategy Paper (IPRSP) and the Universal Basic Education programme.[9] There are plans to hold additional workshops in order to develop gender Action Plans for five more states.

Yemen offers another example of the Partnership adding value to the approaches of the partner agencies. The World Bank has the largest externally funded education programme in Yemen, and UNICEF is implementing it. The Partnership is just beginning activities there to facilitate dialogue on girls' education between the key donors, including DFID, the Dutch and German governments, and several large private-sector companies. This is an opportunity for the Partnership to influence education programmes at an early stage, ensuring that donors' approaches are harmonised, with gender equity mainstreamed into them throughout.

The Partnership is also adding value to UNICEF's gender training programme. UNICEF is developing training modules for UNGEI and has sought technical input from the World Bank and DFID. The aim is to produce training resources which can be used for a broad range of stakeholders, including donors, government, and civil-society groups. The potential benefit of collaboratively produced gender training materials is that they can foster a shared understanding of gender inequalities among various stakeholders and help to bring about consensus on how to address inequalities within specific national contexts.

One of the important factors in the Partnership's success is its access to the in-country staff of each of the partner organisations – and, through them, to governments, the broader donor community, and sources of critical information. This allows the Partnership to be closely involved in mainstream policy processes, such as sector-wide approaches and PRSPs, to ensure that gender-equity policies are adopted and then implemented.

However, the fact that the Partnership exists at the Secretariat level as a separate entity and is not integrated into a geographical desk means that extra efforts have to be made to work through country programmes. There is a risk of isolation for gender programmes that are stand-alone units, institutionally separate from a geographical division – a common problem in governments where the Ministry of Women's Affairs, for example, may not have a sufficient budget or easy access to other line ministries. A separate gender unit within an organisation can work effectively, if mandated to work across all programmes. This has been a difficulty for the Partnership, in that its country work has often been made possible through opportunities in country programmes where individuals are committed to gender equity. There has been strong co-ordination nevertheless between Partnership representatives and agency staff in some countries. Depending on the activity or the context, in-country decision making has often been a collaborative effort between partnership representatives, in-country agency staff, and partner governments.

As is clear from some of its activities, the Partnership has aligned much of its work with Bank-funded programmes – for example in Ecuador, Egypt, Nigeria, and Yemen. Involvement in these programmes and activities has strengthened the Partnership's ability to make gender equity a priority. The World Bank is the largest education-funding agency; because of this, it is often one of the most influential partners in developing countries. By working to mainstream sound gender-equity policies into the Bank's education initiatives, the Partnership has an opportunity to deliver great gains for girls' education at the national level. While working with the World Bank is clearly essential, it is important to prevent the Partnership being seen as solely a World Bank effort. Most likely, as the Partnership becomes responsive to other key players at the country level, and as it links more closely with other agencies, this over-identification with the Bank will no longer be the case.

The challenges of close collaboration

While the successes of a highly collaborative partnership are demonstrated by the activities described above, they do bring their own challenges, because they require a degree of commitment that can be difficult for partners to maintain. In 2003, the Partnership commissioned a review of its activities and structures which generated some helpful insights into the challenges faced and the strategies for addressing them.[10] In particular, the review reveals the lessons to be learned from the Partnership on how to work well together.

One of the challenges to the Partnership comes from the collaboration between three very different organisations – a UN institution, an international lending organisation, and a bilateral development agency. Representatives come to the Partnership from institutions which have different agendas and function in different ways (not to mention the differing institutional cultures and histories within which each representative works). As in all partnership engagements, participants need to balance the objectives and expectations of the partnership and those of their own institutions. Bringing these organisations together to collaborate successfully has been an achievement in itself. All the representatives are equally committed to the gender-equity goals for education and have overcome institutional differences by building strong personal relationships. The informal relationships between representatives seem to have been essential to making the Partnership work.

Another early lesson from the Partnership is that building trust through effective communication is important. But it is a challenge, because sustaining relationships and maintaining communication involve large investments of time. When representatives have to respond to competing demands, it can mean that commitment and engagement are affected. Such complex relationships also place greater organisational demands on the Secretariat. The Partnership review suggests addressing these challenges in various ways, including use of the website as a vehicle for communication between partners. It also suggests that partner agencies should explicitly discuss the areas on which they wish to focus.

Again the informal nature of interactions and decision making has been to the advantage of the Partnership. It has not only cultivated trust and openness between the partners: it has also allowed the Partnership to operate in a flexible and responsive way, which has been a significant factor in its success on the ground. Avoiding a bureaucratic and formal approach is a good lesson for partnerships, as there is a risk of becoming dominated by internal processes, with a loss of flexibility and the capacity to act quickly.

Degrees of participation and power in decision making within the Partnership are not determined by financial resources. What makes the Partnership distinctive is that it is a highly collaborative initiative, in which all partners have an equal voice. While it is obvious that financial resources are necessary to carry forward activities, partners are expected to contribute technical expertise too. Partners' knowledge, experience, and commitment are assets that are quite as significant to the Partnership as are financial resources. In most multi-donor partnerships, those without resources are excluded, and those contributing the most money implicitly have the most power and influence in decision-making processes. The Partnership challenges this logic, operating on alternative, more inclusive principles. Because the Partnership is committed to a high degree of collaboration in informing and influencing national processes to improve conditions for girls, its core resources are knowledge and expertise.

Further expansion of the Partnership is being considered. According to the Partnership Secretariat, several other bilateral agencies and companies in the private sector have asked to join it. Expansion can bring both opportunities and challenges. On the one hand, scaling up brings new ideas. Including more partners means broader collaboration and more voices to support the achievement of the 2005 MDG. It also increases the resources available to the Partnership, enabling it to maintain its responsiveness and engage in activities in more countries. New partners are expected to invest in the Partnership – whether in the form of technical support, staff, or financial contributions – and to be actively involved in activities and decision-making.

On the other hand, an expanded Partnership poses the challenge of achieving consensus, as new partners bring in their own organisational priorities and approaches. Also, communication and consultation would be even more time-consuming, which could result in slower decision-making processes. Retaining flexibility and responsiveness could be more difficult in a Partnership with more members. But if the same level of personal relationships and trust can be maintained with informal communication structures, the Partnership could in fact become even more responsive to emerging needs and opportunities.

Conclusion

Several lessons can be drawn from the UNICEF/World Bank/DFID Partnership on Sustainable Strategies for Girls' Education. The Partnership brings together three very different agencies, building on each one's comparative advantage, and catalysing co-operation where it had not previously existed. This type of highly collaborative partnership is unique among multi-donor partnerships. It is a complex endeavour, because collaboration makes demands of all partners. Thus far, the Partnership has succeeded through building strong personal relationships and maintaining informal interactions, and through mediation between partners which fosters understanding of the 'home' institutional culture of each member. But all this requires time, commitment, and trust.

While it is too early to judge the long-term impact of the Partnership, there are some evident early successes which suggest a model for strong partnerships for girls' education.

- Flexible and responsive structures which allow partners to move quickly on demand and to meet opportunities as they arise.
- High-quality analytical work which fills the gaps in data for sound gender-equity policy making.
- Working within mainstream processes to bring key stakeholders together to discuss the evidence and agree on the best policy decisions.
- Acting as a catalyst in the policy-making process, developing momentum for sustained action.
- Disseminating the lessons learned.

The challenges of this model are considerable, as they are for any partnership that involves a high level of commitment. It remains to be seen how that commitment will be sustained, and what the impact will be on the ground. But the potential of co-ordinated joint efforts is much more promising than that of individual initiatives.

Adaeze Igboemeka works for the Education For All Team of the UK government's Department for International Development, specialising in gender equity and rights issues in education. She has worked as a consultant on higher-education issues for the Swedish International Development and Co-operation Agency (SIDA) and was a lecturer at Eduardo Mondlane University in Maputo, Mozambique.

Notes

1   This paper draws on a review of Partnership documents, and discussions with Rachel Hinton (DFID), Carolyn Winter (World Bank), Laure Beaufils (DFID), and Nick Dossetor (DFID). At the time of writing there was no UNICEF representative in place with the Partnership.

2   The author is assistant education adviser at DFID.

3   Since this chapter was written, many of the Partnership's functions have in fact been transferred to UNGEI. Others have become the responsibility of the 'Beyond Access' Project, a collaboration between the UK government, the London University Institute of Education, and Oxfam GB.

4   Poverty Reduction Strategy Papers (PRSPs) describe a country's macro-economic, structural, and social policies and programmes to promote growth and reduce poverty. They are prepared by governments through a participatory process involving civil society and development partners.

5   'Pioneering Support for Girls' Secondary Education: The Bangladesh Female Secondary School Assistance Project' (1999),The World Bank Group.

6   For access to other studies on Bangladesh, see the Publications search page at www.girlseducation.org/PGE_Active_Pages/Resources/Publications/b-right.asp

7   Patrick J. McEwan and Wilson Jiménez (2002), 'Indigenous Students in Bolivian Primary Schools: Patterns and Determinants of Inequities', www.girlseducation.org/PGE_Active_Pages/NewsAndEvents/main.asp

8   Cf. Henrietta Miers and Janet Seeley (2003), 'Some Recent Examples in Gender Mainstreaming in DFID', draft, DFID.

9   For the workshop reports and supporting documents, see: www.girlseducation.org/PGE_Active_Pages/NewsAndEvents/b-right2.asp?Action=Display HTML&FileName=34

10   Beryl A. Radin (2003), 'The Partnership for Sustainable Strategies on Girls' Education: Progress to Date and Moving Forward'.

3 Pressure from within: the Forum for African Women Educationalists

Penina Mlama

The provision and quality of girls' education in sub-Saharan Africa (SSA) have attracted increasing attention over the past decade. The World Conference on Education For All (EFA), held in Jomtien in 1990, set the year 2000 as the target for reaching its goal. The Forum for African Women Educationalists (FAWE), created as a response to this challenge, has been at the forefront of promoting girls' education on the continent. This chapter illustrates how FAWE has proceeded to fulfil its mandate, the challenges that it has faced, and the crucial role played by partnerships in the implementation of its programmes.

The status of girls' education in sub-Saharan Africa

According to available evidence, investment in female education in low-income countries of Africa is a 'best bet' investment which simultaneously achieves greater earning ability for families, lower fertility rates, reduced rates of infant and maternal mortality, and improvements in public health. Investment in female education is a regenerative process which produces continuing generations of children who are ready to learn and engage in behaviour which supports a wide range of national development goals.

Despite dramatic gains in enrolment over the past 30 years, statistics still present a grim picture of the education of African women and girls. According to the EFA Global Monitoring Report released in November 2003, of 11 developing countries around the world where girls have 20 per cent less chance of starting school than boys, seven are in sub-Saharan Africa (SSA). Half of the countries with a net enrolment ratio (NER) between 60 per cent and 80 per cent are African, while a further 14 countries in SSA have NERs below 60 per cent. With 23 million girls out of school, SSA ranks lower than any other region. Many factors continue to keep vast numbers of girls out of the classroom in this region; among them are poverty, long-held negative attitudes to women's intellectual capabilities, teenage pregnancy, early marriage, insensitive school environments, examination failure – particularly in mathematics, science, and technology – and traditional divisions of labour.

FAWE: origins, structure, and activities

Origins

FAWE is a pan-African non-government organisation which brings together senior women policy makers in the education sector who are committed to improving girls' education. Its origins date back to 1991, when concerned observers realised that Africa was moving too slowly towards implementation of the 1990 EFA declaration, given the many millions of African girls who had no hope of gaining an education unless concerted efforts were made.

Five women ministers of education from Africa attended a meeting of World Bank donors to African education in Manchester, England, in October 1991. They were Hon. Simone Tesa (Seychelles); Hon. Alice Tiendrebeogo (Burkina Faso); Hon. Paulete Moussavon-Missambo (Gabon); Hon. Fay Chung (Zimbabwe); and Hon. Vida Yeboah (Ghana). They held an informal meeting to review the seemingly intractable problems that confront women and girls aspiring to education and development in the African continent. With an analysis of these problems, the group believed strongly that there was much that they themselves and others in decision-making positions could do to improve the situation. They mooted the idea of establishing a panel of prominent African women educationalists to act as a think-tank and pressure-group, to stimulate action to improve education for girls and women in Africa. This pressure-group became the nucleus of FAWE, which is a much larger formal network, designed to combine individual strengths in order to influence educational policy in the continent. FAWE was registered in 1993 in Kenya, where it established its regional secretariat. Today, FAWE comprises eight cabinet ministers and more than 60 other high-level women educators in the 32 countries in sub-Saharan Africa where it has national chapters.

Membership

FAWE's greatest asset is its membership. It has engaged an impressive array of senior educationalists and policy makers as members over the last ten years, nurturing their mutual support, collaboration, intellectual dialogue, and capacity building in the context of furthering its mission. FAWE membership has three categories:

- Full members: serving women ministers of education, vice-chancellors, and other prominent women in education. These women, who constitute the core of FAWE's General Assembly, are entitled to participate and vote in all the deliberations of FAWE. In 2003, full members represented 34 African countries.

- Associate members: male ministers of education and male vice-chancellors, as well as donors and organisations working on girls' education and development, who form strategic partnerships with FAWE.

- FAWE national chapters: established in 32 sub-Saharan African countries, national chapters ensure the effective evaluation of the status of girls' education at national level and the implementation of FAWE's mission. They draw their own memberships from various levels and sectors of education and development in the countries concerned.

These three structures form a network that is co-ordinated by a small secretariat based in Nairobi. The secretariat ensures the day-to-day management of the organisation, provides coherence of direction in policy and programme activities, and ensures the monitoring and evaluation of FAWE's programme.

Activities

FAWE has created and sustained partnerships with governments, donors, NGOs, universities, communities, the media, and other stakeholders in education to promote positive attitudes, policies, and practices that will transform education systems to ensure equity for girls. FAWE has four main strategic objectives:

- Influencing policy formulation, planning, and implementation in favour of increasing access, improving retention, and enhancing the performance of girls.

- Promoting public awareness and consensus on the social and economic advantages of girls' education.

- Demonstrating, through practical interventions, how to achieve increased access for girls, improved retention, and better performance.

- Influencing replication and mainstreaming of best practices from the demonstration interventions into national education policy and practice.

Influencing policy

FAWE's highly influential membership, operating at various levels with a multiplicity of partners, has enabled it to influence education policy and to carry out an effective advocacy programme which has ensured that girls' education is increasingly being incorporated into the heart of governments' sectoral programmes, besides remaining high on the agenda of education ministries. However, sustaining this membership and its commitment is a big challenge, because of the fluidity of ministerial appointments and other senior government positions in sub-Saharan Africa. Constant government reshuffles and shifting political alignments impair the effectiveness of this partnership, because partners' influence may diminish as they move outside their former sphere of operation.

A major concern for FAWE has been to ensure that the national EFA action plans and policies are gender-responsive. This is one of the activities under the FAWE / UNICEF joint programme, as stipulated in a memorandum of understanding signed in 2001. This has involved organising capacity-building programmes for national teams to help them to lobby effectively for reform and skilfully guide the mainstreaming of gender into the EFA process. As part of this crucial exercise, FAWE developed a tool, the *ABC of Gender Responsive Education Policies – Guidelines for Analysis and Planning,* which is a step-by-step process of analysing education policies and plans for gender responsiveness, and presenting the principles of gender mainstreaming. As a result of this collaboration, a number of countries have paid more attention to gender in their EFA national action plans. This has been revealed by an on-going analysis of country action plans by FAWE, as mandated by UNESCO / BREDA. To date, FAWE has analysed action plans from 17 countries. Another result of this partnership is that a number of FAWE national chapters have been actively involved as members of various committees, task forces, and other specialist groups concerned with encouraging the EFA process.

Many other challenges constrain FAWE's partnership with government ministries of education. One is the insufficiency of the resources allocated to the process of formulating the national action plans, and the similar under-funding of specific local initiatives to support girls' education. Another challenge is the lack of sufficient capacity in ministries of education to translate gender awareness into action. Many middle-level government officials engaged in the actual formulation of education policies and plans, although aware of gender issues, may not have the technical capacity for gender analysis or main-streaming. Concern about gender inequality therefore will not translate into gender-responsive policies and plans – and this is the reason why FAWE has put so much emphasis on capacity building for gender equity in its partnership with government ministries. The goal is to ensure that these middle-level policy makers are as aware and sensitised as the ministers of education themselves, since their work is essential in articulating gender equity throughout the planning and implementation process.

Another challenge is the lack of capacity of FAWE's national chapters to position their interventions strategically within the mainstream of national policies and processes such as Poverty Reduction Strategy Papers, Education For All, and the Fast Track Initiative for education.

FAWE knows that the interest of male ministers of education and heads of state who have been enlisted as FAWE associate members must be continuously reinvigorated and nurtured. FAWE will not only continue to strengthen these partnerships through its traditional channels, such as ministerial consultations and its General Assembly platforms, but will also actively participate in newer EFA forums, such as the New Partnership for Africa's Development (NEPAD) and the newly launched Forum for African Parliamentarians in Education (FAPED).

Advocacy

FAWE's advocacy is based on data from research projects on the determinants of female participation in education. This initial research, which spanned 23 countries in Africa, was undertaken in partnership with the African Academy of Sciences and 11 donors. The accumulated data formed the basis of FAWE's advocacy to re-invigorate political commitment to EFA goals and to increase public awareness of the benefits of girls' education for development. FAWE has engaged in a wide range of activities and produced advocacy materials in numerous formats, including an award-winning film, 'These Girls are Missing' (Michael Camerini), on the subject of family decision-making on investment in daughters' education. Another example is FAWE's Best Practices Series, which identifies and documents successful examples of strategies which work on the ground to overcome obstacles to girls' education. FAWE's aim is to disseminate these materials to education policy makers, in order to encourage the mainstreaming and replication of its interventions. Some of the interventions described in the Best Practices Series include the following:

- Providing bursaries to girls from poor households.
- Facilitating re-entry for girls who are out of school for reasons of pregnancy and childcare.
- Creating Centres of Excellence.
- Empowering girls.
- Supporting peer counselling on the subject of HIV/AIDS.
- Providing education for girls in conflict-affected areas.
- Addressing issues of sexual maturation.

FAWE and UNICEF, under a Memorandum of Understanding signed in July 2001, have acted in partnership in a variety of activities to advocate improvements in girls' education. The two organisations have worked closely in the implementation of both the African Girls' Education Initiative (AGEI) and the UN Girls' Education Initiative (UNGEI), and indeed FAWE has now merged with the latter. UNICEF is still one of the major programmatic partners for FAWE national chapters. It has made valuable contributions to the collaborative programmes to improve access, retention, and performance of girls at school. UNICEF has supported activities such as media workshops in Senegal and Gabon; capacity building in advocacy for FAWE members in Tanzania, Zimbabwe, and Guinea; and support for the launch of the Girls' Education Movement (GEM) in Tanzania, among others. In August 2001, UNICEF collaborated with FAWE and its Uganda chapter to launch the GEM. Since then, FAWE chapters in Tanzania and Zambia have launched GEM in their own countries.

Demonstration interventions

Another major activity for FAWE has been demonstration interventions. A number of projects illustrating how to set up and manage holistic models of girls' education have been undertaken.

Female Education in Mathematics and Science in Africa (FEMSA)

This intervention was designed to strengthen the participation of girls in science, mathematics, and technology and to encourage Ministries of Education and policy makers to make the necessary adjustments in curriculum design, teacher-training courses, and examinations policy to ensure girl students' fuller participation and better achievement. The project ran for six years (1995–2001), co-ordinated jointly with NORAD and supported by seven donors. Twelve countries participated: Burkina Faso, Cameroon, Kenya, Malawi, Mali, Mozambique, Senegal, Swaziland, Tanzania, Uganda, and Zambia. These interventions were implemented in 123 government schools, reaching an estimated grassroots population of one million people across Africa.

The FEMSA project generated a number of innovative practices that are now being implemented in 10 countries in sub-Saharan Africa, for example science camps for girls, and local production of teaching and learning materials.

The NGO Alliance for Community Action in Girls' Education, and the Agathe Uwilingiyimana Prize

Both these programmes aimed to empower indigenous civil-society organisations to play an increasing role in supporting education, especially that of girls. Through the NGO Alliance, 200 NGOs and community-based organisations (CBOs) in five countries were involved in capacity building and networking, while more than 50 of them received seed grants to support girls' education projects. The Alliance did much to open up greater space for civil-society organisations to increase their level of responsibility and ownership of education at the grassroots level.

The Agathe Uwilingiyimana Prize, in memory of the late Rwandan Prime Minister, a FAWE member, has to date been given to 23 NGO / CBOs for innovative programmes in support of girls' education. Communities are encouraged to identify potential recipients of the award. Part of the prize is to be spent on documenting programmes and increasing their impact, by making links with policy makers and funding agencies. The fund is administered through FAWE's national chapters. Training and other support required for the replication and mainstreaming of successful strategies is provided by FAWE.

The effectiveness of the national chapters is limited in many cases by inadequate structures and capacity for good governance, programme implementation, monitoring and evaluation, and resource mobilisation. Many also lack the capacity to operate at the grassroots level. Constant attention must be given to strengthening the national chapters, since they are the engines that drive FAWE's work on the ground.

Partnership in practice

If girls' access to education is increased, and if, once they enter school, they receive a good-quality education within an environment where they feel welcome and valued, they will be motivated to progress through primary school to acquire basic intellectual and practical skills, perform well, and complete the cycle with a level of achievement which enables them to advance to higher levels of education. If FAWE is to respond to this multifaceted challenge in a focused and effective manner, it will need partners who understand gender equity, who are well informed, and who can remain enthusiastic and committed.

FAWE's Centres of Excellence

FAWE has learned over the years that it is one thing to identify and create partnerships – and quite another to ensure that such partners understand girls' education issues and that they are willing and able to contribute to providing solutions to the many problems that beset girls' education. FAWE's response to this need, in partnership with a variety of key stakeholders, has been to demonstrate how to convert ordinary public schools into Centres of Excellence.

A FAWE Centre of Excellence (CoE) is a school which clearly and effectively demonstrates a holistic, integrated approach to the task of improving girls' educational opportunities, by creating an enabling environment for learning and teaching. It is a school which is gender-responsive in all its aspects, including the physical infrastructure, the social environment, and the academic environment. Today, FAWE CoEs are operating in six countries: The Gambia, Kenya, Namibia, Rwanda, Senegal, and Tanzania. There is a total of eight centres, with Kenya and Tanzania hosting two each.

The programme recognises that there are many participants who can make a key contribution to the creation of an enabling environment for good-quality education for girls. They include students, teachers, school managers, ministries of education and other line ministries, parents, communities, communications media, and donors. Their involvement can be enhanced through two key strategies: first, by building a strong partnership of all these players; and second, by ensuring capacity building for each category, to equip them for effective sustenance of the programme. Another feature is the recognition that specific inputs – ranging from physical and material infrastructure to programmes for enhancing the social, physical, psychological, and emotional development of girls – are important in providing a safe learning environment which is conducive to achieving academic excellence. The intervention package in a CoE programme includes the following elements.

- Capacity building for teachers, to increase their awareness of gender-related issues.
- Gender-responsive teaching methodologies and classroom interaction.
- Programmes to enhance girls' academic performance and develop critical thinking and problem-solving skills.
- Empowerment programmes to increase the assertiveness and confidence of both girls and boys.
- Physical infrastructure to ensure a safe and secure environment for girls.
- Guidance and counselling services to cater for girls' psychological and emotional development.
- Special attention to the needs of female students who are at risk of dropping out of school for reasons of poverty.
- A gender-responsive school-management system.
- Sensitisation of the community to support girls' education.
- Involvement of all stakeholders in the development and implementation of the programme.
- Close collaboration and partnership with the ministry of education in the implementation of the programme.
- Documentation and dissemination of the best practices employed by the CoE.

Investment in a CoE is a major undertaking which requires input from many stakeholders, whose interest in and sense of ownership of the project must be developed and sustained. For FAWE this is a big challenge, which must be confronted head-on if gender issues are to be addressed centrally. Some specific examples are discussed in the section below.

Partnerships with education ministries

FAWE recognises that the ministry of education (MoE) in each country is the entity with primary responsibility for providing education for its citizens. The MoE must therefore be FAWE's key partner in its efforts to demonstrate how to convert an ordinary school into a CoE. Moreover, the ministry is responsible for mainstreaming and replicating the model in the rest of the country.

The CoE, right from the outset, is designed as a joint venture between the FAWE Secretariat, the FAWE national chapter, and the MoE. A Memorandum of Understanding, clearly stating the responsibility of each partner, supports this venture. As one of its first duties, the ministry is expected, for example, to provide data – both qualitative and quantitative – on the status of education, as well as socio-economic parameters to guide the selection of the school to be converted to a CoE. It is also expected to maintain its responsibility for recruitment and payment of teachers' salaries, provision of all the basic elements such as infrastructure, and the supply of teaching and learning materials.

For FAWE, one major problem is the fact that economic hardships limit the ability of most African governments to maintain schools at the required minimum standards. Often schools lack the basic infrastructure that an ordinary school should have. Often FAWE has had to upgrade some elements of a school system or structure to bring it to the level of a standard ordinary public school, before starting to convert it into a CoE.

In over-worked ministries, the value of girls' education is usually under-emphasised, a fact which leads to delays in implementing activities accepted by the ministry during consultative meetings. FAWE has experienced many initial problems in its partnership with ministries of education: for example, haphazard transfers of teachers from CoEs in which FAWE has invested heavily in skills development; delays in recruitment of teachers; and poor remuneration for teachers. An effective partnership between FAWE and a MoE would require the ministry to commit itself to doing the following:

- Develop the infrastructure of its schools at least to the level required of an ordinary school.
- Accept and act on the fact that the quality of girls' education cannot be improved without addressing the task from a gender-aware perspective.

- Review education plans and policies for gender responsiveness, and include strategies that will enhance the quality of girls' education.

- Allocate specific and additional resources to ensure a gender-responsive environment in all schools.

- Train teachers and school administrators in gender responsiveness.

- Replicate the Centre of Excellence model as a way of improving the quality of schooling for both girls and boys.

Community partnerships in Centres of Excellence

A supportive and active community is an indispensable partner in any programme designed to improve girls' education, because most of the problems faced by girls in schools stem from conditions in the home and the community. Schools are often isolated enclaves, lacking links with the community; but FAWE's experience of managing CoEs has shown that local communities can break down what may seem like insurmountable obstacles, if they are convinced of the resulting benefits.

The community has to be fully sensitised to understand the importance of girls' education. It should be involved in identifying local factors that constrain efforts to provide it; appreciate how the proposed programme would respond to these issues; and be able to recognise the importance of its own role and contribution to the success of this programme. For FAWE, one way to do this is its *Vision Workshops*, which are typically the starting point for marshalling support for the intervention from all the various stakeholders. These workshops employ a participatory learning approach, incorporating drama as a way of identifying problems and their solutions. Participants in these workshops have come out feeling that they have a stake in both the CoE process and its outcomes. Individualised follow-up sessions aim to build the capacity of specific partners, to enrich their contribution to the CoE.

Communities in the existing CoEs have proved very supportive in significant ways. For example, they have supported the building of additional classrooms, laboratories, libraries, and teachers' houses. In some cases, community leaders have taken it upon themselves to sensitise parents to the benefits of sending their daughters to schools, and to discourage early marriages, a common reason why many girls drop out of school. In a number of CoEs, communities have raised funds for scholarship schemes.

In its collaboration with local communities, FAWE has sometimes had to deal with deeply entrenched cultural beliefs which militate against girls' education. Cultural practices such as female genital mutilation and early marriage are deeply entrenched among the Maasai of Kenya, where FAWE has one of its centres: the African Inland Church girls' school. In the medium term, such practices will continue to conflict with the message of the CoEs and will require the combined efforts of all the stakeholders to find ways of combating them. Other challenges relate to 'felt needs' that are not directly education-related; for example, income-generation projects for poor families to enable them to support their children's school expenses; mediation between parents and daughters who are threatened with forced marriages; and input into policies on teachers' terms and conditions of service that are the direct responsibility of the MoE.

Partnerships with teachers and school managers

Teachers' contributions to educational partnerships are limited by a wide range of factors, including poor training and remuneration, the impacts of HIV/AIDS, lack of gender awareness, and the absence of a clearly defined school-management system. These difficulties all too often create a feeling of despondency and lack of interest in the profession, which is increasingly considered by most teachers as a job of last resort, a temporary occupation during the search for more lucrative alternative employment.

FAWE has organised capacity-building programmes for teachers in CoEs on topics such as gender-responsive teaching methodologies (especially for science, mathematics, and technology), guidance and counselling, and school self-evaluation. Through these programmes, teachers have sharpened their teaching skills and have had opportunities to meet and share experiences with teachers from other countries, thus partly overcoming the extreme professional isolation suffered by teachers in sub-Saharan Africa. Such programmes are of significant motivational value for teachers, and they promote a healthy teacher/student relationship.

These programmes can be costly, and it is only through partnerships that FAWE can implement them. For example, 51 teachers from CoEs in Rwanda, Kenya, and Tanzania took part in a programme on school self-evaluation, jointly organised by FAWE and the Commonwealth Secretariat (Leader of the Association for the Development of Education in Africa (ADEA) Working Group on the Teaching Professions) in Nairobi in 2001. The programme was designed to enable teachers to participate in the process of evaluating their own schools' performance and to contribute to subsequent planning for improvements.

Partnerships with boys and girls

FAWE recognises that an effective teaching methodology is one which involves the active participation of the learners. For girls' participation to improve, they need to be empowered to overcome the lack of self-confidence and competitiveness and the fear of speaking out in public that result from traditional African socialisation processes. FAWE has devised a package of activities to improve the participation of girls in learning, and to prevent them from dropping out of school: scholarship awards for girls from poor families; the provision of boarding facilities; remedial classes to improve girls' academic performance; interaction with peer educators; science clubs; and empowerment programmes (round-table discussions, role-model programmes, drama projects, and girls' club activities) to help girls to protect themselves against HIV/AIDS and sexual harassment. It has been found that programmes designed to empower girls also benefit boys in co-educational settings.

A particular challenge confronting FAWE is how to deal with the impacts of HIV/AIDs on learning: for example, the stigma and fear experienced by girls whose parents are sick; the expectation that girls will drop out of school to support their orphaned siblings; and the fear and trauma experienced by school children when they learn that their teacher has AIDS.

Empowering girls to assert their rights can create problems for their teachers, who need support to prepare them to work without anxiety in an environment which supports democracy and empowers students to speak out on issues that affect them, including poor teaching or sexual harassment. FAWE is also increasingly recognising that boys (and the community as a whole) need to be involved in similar programmes, to prepare them for the changes that will be wrought by empowered girls in their own homes.

Partnerships with donors and other support groups

Human, financial, and material resources are all required by the establishment of Centres of Excellence. Ministries of education are the main providers of schooling and are bearing the main costs of the CoEs, since they are government schools. Communities have contributed significantly in terms of mobilising resources. Donor partners, mainly those in the FAWE donor consortium (the governments of Norway and Finland, the Rockefeller Foundation, the World Bank, Swedish International Development Co-operation Agency [SIDA], Ireland Aid, UNICEF, USAID/Advance Africa, and UNESCO) have contributed to FAWE's work, thus enabling interventions on the ground.

Challenges

Keeping partnerships engaged and involved

The strength of FAWE's 32 national chapters begins with the rich diversity and commitment of their membership – and therein lies a challenge for FAWE. Nurturing and sustaining this diverse membership, which ranges from cabinet ministers to local community leaders, from vice-chancellors to primary teachers, from parents to girls themselves, is a big challenge. Yet recognising the central role that must be played by national chapters to achieve its goals, FAWE is committed to ensuring that the chapters grow into professional organisations, fully competent to develop programmes and implement specific interventions that will demonstrate ways of ensuring girls' access, retention, and achievement. FAWE therefore provides a diverse capacity-building programme, ranging from skills required to run an effective national chapter to skills of promoting the retention, performance, and achievement of girls in schools. All the national chapters run courses on writing funding proposals, strategic planning, advocacy techniques, monitoring and evaluation, gender equity, guidance and counselling, and computer skills.

Maintaining clarity of purpose

Through a series of capacity-building workshops, FAWE has trained national teams to work with government policy makers and other stakeholders in the process of applying gender analysis and mainstreaming gender-related concerns in education policy and plans, especially the EFA National Action Plans. As these teams have worked with various stakeholders, from senior policy makers to grassroots community representatives, they have had to deal with the various perceptions, definitions, and conceptions of the word 'gender'. To compound this problem, it has been difficult to maintain the tempo and enthusiasm of some key stakeholders for any initiative associated with gender equity.

Sustaining partnerships in gender mainstreaming at the national level works well where the activity is part and parcel of the on-going work-plan of the ministry of education, rather than depending on the interest and enthusiasm of individuals. In some countries, reshuffles and transfers of staff within the MoE have halted or reversed the EFA process, as enthusiastic officers are moved, and their places are taken by new staff who have little interest in the process.

Maintaining clarity of vision

An on-going analysis of EFA national action plans, based on a mandate given to FAWE by UNESCO / BREDA, has produced some interesting results. The 17 countries analysed so far have, in general, done a commendable job in mainstreaming gender into the EFA National Action Plans (NAPs). However, it was noted that in most cases the initiatives were not sufficient to achieve gender parity and gender equality in time to meet the deadlines set at the Dakar conference. The analysis revealed that the countries that participated in the FAWE capacity-building programmes had mainstreamed more gender-related activities in their NAPs, which indicates that these countries had a clearer vision of the potential value of girls' education; were able to identify actual problems created by gender discrimination in schools; and were therefore more likely to suggest appropriate strategies for interventions.

Mobilising resources

Efforts to establish, consolidate, and nurture partnerships with a variety of organisations interested in girls' education require costly investments of funds and time. Resources must be set aside to sustain capacity-building programmes for partners such as teachers and others in the national chapters with responsibility for promoting girls' education at the grassroots. Bursaries for girls from poor families require funds, as do sustained empowerment activities to improve girls' academic performance; regular sensitisation of community members on their role in girls' education; and advocacy through active participation in meetings and other forums.

Monitoring and evaluation

Monitoring and evaluation of the effectiveness of partnerships are necessary in order to ensure that all members share the same goals and are sustaining their optimum level and quality of performance. FAWE therefore keeps all its partners well informed of the development and progress of activities geared towards improvement of girls' education. This is done through forums like the FAWE General Assembly, held every three years, publications like the annual report, the institute's quarterly newsletter, *FAWE News*, and the FAWE website. However, many of the FAWE partners, particularly those at the grassroots, lack the skills and infrastructure necessary for effective communication.

Conclusion

Research has shown that the challenge of improving girls' education is multi-faceted and requires a variety of solutions. Partnerships are necessary, because so many participants are involved in making girls' education work: girls and boys, teachers, parents, community leaders, educational professionals and administrators, communications media, and others. They are all essential cogs in the wheel that keeps girls' education moving forwards. Understanding the concept of gender equity and the role expected of each partner in improving the situation of girls and women is crucial. Also important are adequate resources and effective strategies for communication between partners, in order to keep everyone engaged and informed.

Although partnerships have increased between FAWE and national governments, donors, and civil society, more effort is required to share experiences and to identify and document the best practices that can enrich the nationwide strategies to eliminate gender disparities in education. So for FAWE the creation and nurturing of strong and effective partnerships in the promotion of girls' education in Africa will continue to be a major goal. This is the only way of successfully addressing the multiple constraints facing girls and women in Africa, if the goals of Education For All are to be met.

Dr Penina Mlama, formerly a professor at the University of Dar es Salaam, is currently the Executive Director of the Forum for African Women Educationalists (FAWE).

Sources and further reading

Association for the Development of Education in Africa (ADEA) (2003) 'The Quest For Quality in Girls' Education', ADEA Biennial, Mauritius. Monitoring Report 2003/4, Paris: UNESCO.

FAWE (2000, 2001, 2002) Annual Reports, Nairobi: FAWE.

FAWE (2000) 'Closing the gender gap in education: curbing dropout', *FAWE News* Vol. 8 No. 3.

FAWE (2001) 'In Search of An Ideal School for Girls. FAWE Centres of Excellence', Nairobi: FAWE.

FAWE (2001) 'Creating an enabling environment for girls in school', *FAWE News* Vol. 9 No. 1.

FAWE (2002) 'Education For All: FAWE's action at the grassroots', *FAWE News* Vol. 10 Nos. 1 & 2.

FAWE (2003) 'Girls' Education in Africa. Promoting Partnership for Action on the Ground', FAWE Revised Strategic Direction 2002–2006, Nairobi: FAWE.

FAWE (2003) 'Mission to Evaluate FEMSA Activities', Nairobi: FAWE.

UNESCO (2003) *Gender and Education For All: the Leap to Equality*, EFA Global Monitoring Report.

Part Two
Discourse and Practice

4 Emerging partnerships in the Philippine EFA process

Rene R. Raya and Raquel de Guzman Castillo

Education has always been a significant issue, and often a contentious one, in the Philippines. At least in part this is due to the fact that a large number of civil-society organisations in the country trace their inception to the militant movement of students, youth, and teachers that figured prominently in the education-reform movement of the 1960s and 1970s. Such organisations began engaging with very specific issues of student rights, tuition fees, teachers' welfare, academic freedom, and other campus-related concerns. The struggles then gradually shifted to broader political issues, and soon schools became the bastions of the anti-dictatorship struggle, which dominated the themes of the Philippine socio-political movements until the mid-1980s.

The fall of the Marcos dictatorship in 1986 and developments in the international arena brought about a period of transition in the civil-society movement in the Philippines. New issues were brought forward, and various NGOs emerged to take up new challenges. NGOs also became more flexible in their engagement with the government.

This chapter considers the transition experienced in the relationship between the government and civil-society organisations (CSOs) working in education. It illustrates how the nature of the engagement has shifted from a confrontational approach to one characterised by co-operation (although CSOs still strive to maintain their critical edge). We will also show that, despite this, the transition has been long and painful, and a genuine partnership between government and CSOs has still to emerge.

On a more positive note, we conclude by arguing that the experience of partnership among CSOs has largely been a positive one, with coalitions and alliances being formed to link individual sectoral initiatives and to gain strength and impact through co-ordinated advocacy. The formation and activities of the Civil Society Network for Education Reforms (Education Network, or E-Net) are major examples of this evolution. New alliances have taken active roles in the areas of rural development, environment conservation, social development, human-rights education, and governance. Other NGOs have focused their efforts on the disadvantaged and marginalised groups in society.

In this context, gender work in education was led by organisations with programmes in literacy and alternative learning systems which have long engaged with government on the need to develop appropriate programmes for marginalised women, indigenous peoples, and out-of-school youth. Various women's organisations have consistently campaigned for changes in textbooks and school curricula which are biased against women and girls and prevent their full enjoyment of educational opportunities.

However, as this chapter will show, the issue of girls' education in general has not been a high-priority concern. This is in part because, unlike the reality in other developing countries, national aggregated figures suggest that it is male schoolchildren who are generally under-performing in terms of participation, retention, and achievement of learning competencies.

E-Net and its reform agenda

Relevant to this chapter is a reflection on the weaknesses and strength of civil-society partnerships formed to enact the more comprehensive agenda for Education For All (EFA).

When the EFA project was launched in the Philippines in 1991, associated partnerships were initially characterised by low awareness and weak participation on the part of CSOs. For the most part, CSO participation in the EFA I programme (1991–2000) had been marginal, disjointed, and limited to meetings and collaboration on thematic issues based on the particular mandate and programmes of the concerned organisations. NGOs would later criticise the apparent lack of consultations on the planning and implementation of EFA I. The transition process in the Philippine movement during the late 1980s up to the early 1990s – which will be described later in more detail – is partly to blame.

Far better organised and sustained CSO engagement in the EFA I programme did occur, however, although only in mid-1999 during the latter phase of the EFA I assessment process. Certain external factors helped to stimulate and mobilise Philippine NGOs to engage in the EFA process. In particular, the Education Now campaign of Oxfam International, the lobby initiatives of Education International (EI), and the Global March Against Child Labour served to inspire and support the launching of counterpart activities locally. Oxfam's international campaign was supported by the education advocacy programme initiated by the Manila office of Oxfam Great Britain. Oxfam GB was instrumental in facilitating meetings and dialogues between the government and NGOs which eventually led to the participation of the latter in the EFA assessment process.

While most NGOs perceived their participation in validating the EFA assessment as perfunctory and trivial, their involvement, nonetheless, made them conscious of the need to establish a network to pursue essential reforms in the education sector. The assessment process brought together a range of education-oriented networks and organisations in various forms of partnership. The engagement marked the start of the active participation of CSOs in EFA-related activities. All these contributed to the eventual formation of the Civil Society Network for Education Reforms (Education Network, or E-Net).

E-Net was launched in April 2000 during the national conference on education reforms, attended by more than one hundred organisations involved in education, training, child rights, and related concerns. To date, it is the only existing national coalition that engages with government comprehensively and specifically on the EFA, and consistently brings together other CSOs within the frame of the EFA vision.

The network is guided by the principle that education is a basic human right and an enabling factor. It envisions a Philippine society which provides equitable access to good-quality education that is rights-based, holistic, liberating, and working for the full development of human potential. It is committed to work for education which ensures gender equity, promotes multiculturalism, inculcates active citizenship, and contributes to the attainment of peace, democracy, and development in the country.

E-net is an important example of the kind of partnership in which education-oriented CSOs engage in the Philippines. It fact it serves as a forum for civil society to share ideas and experiences and to engage in joint undertakings to promote its reform agenda and achieve positive changes in education policies and practices.

E-Net did not come about simply as a response to the EFA process. As we have seen, the network traces its origins back to an earlier period and to various organisations and movements that emerged in the 1980s and 1990s. E-Net was instrumental in joining together various groups belonging to the following networks:

- the human-rights movement
- the child-rights network
- NGOs working among at-risk children (street children, abused children, children in situations of armed conflict, trafficked and prostituted children, and child workers)
- the women's movement
- NGOs involved in popular education, development training, and alternative learning systems

- organisations engaged in literacy and education work among indigenous peoples and other disadvantaged groups
- student organisations
- and the teachers' movement.

While most of these groups operate largely outside the school system, they had long been involved in education-related work and advocacy concerns. Child-focused NGOs, for example, emerged as broad and influential networks, especially after the adoption in 1990 of the UN Convention on the Rights of the Child. Many of these groups were directly involved in education services and were instrumental in promoting children's right to good-quality education. Similarly, human-rights organisations in the Philippines broadened their advocacy agenda from one that focused on civil and political rights to a more comprehensive platform which includes economic, social, and political rights.

Since its launch, E-Net has moved forward and transformed itself into a national membership body engaged in advocacy for policy reforms in the education sector. In April 2002, during the EFA Week of Action, E-Net held its first general assembly, attended by around 120 participants representing 100 affiliated organisations nationwide. The assembly refined and substantiated E-Net's reform agenda and formalised its organisational structure. It adopted the Education Reform Agenda and the two-year General Programme of Action. The assembly also elected the Board of Trustees and the National Executive Committee.

E-Net's agenda for policy reform covers four major areas in its immediate two-year general programme: early childhood care and development; formal education; non-formal education and alternative learning systems; and education financing and its monitoring at national and local level. The aims of E-Net's priority programmes and reform measures include the following:

- Ensure the active participation of civil society in education planning and governance and in the pursuit of key education reforms.
- Convene the National Committee on education for all (NCEFA) to institutionalise government and civil-society partnership in EFA planning, implementation, monitoring, and evaluation.
- Work for comprehensive policy reforms to support, improve, and strengthen non-formal education and alternative learning systems.
- Ensure the immediate and full implementation of the new law on early childhood care and development.
- Ensure equitable access to good-quality education for all and adequate attention and support for programmes catering to the needs of vulnerable children, particularly children of poor, ethnic-minority, and marginalised families.

- Promote a gender-fair education system by ensuring parity in access, eliminating gender biases in the school system, and implementing programmes designed specifically for disadvantaged and at-risk girl children.

- Strengthen the democratic structures of governance in the education sector, such as the Local School Boards, by broadening the membership and ensuring the active participation of local communities, families, NGOs, and other stakeholders.

- Reform the school curriculum and develop learning packages that are learner-centred, culture-sensitive, and based on the needs and conditions of specific communities and local areas. The curriculum should promote patriotism, democracy, human rights, peace, and good governance.

- Increase public investment in education by ensuring that education gets the highest budgetary priority in the allocation of national resources.

- Ensure the efficient utilisation of resources and encourage the elimination of corruption in the bureaucracy.

- Strengthen international solidarity to support the EFA goals. Work with UNESCO and other international agencies to facilitate sharing and promote co-operation to meet EFA goals and targets.

In April 2003, E-Net participated in the Week of Action organised by the Global Campaign for Education, a yearly event used by global and regional networks to bring to public attention specific issues and problems in education policy. E-net adopted a theme that focused on peace and education for vulnerable children, especially disadvantaged girls and young women. The week-long activities included a three-day seminar and participation in the world's largest simultaneous lesson: a campaigning effort which involved well over a million people across the world, from rural and urban school children and their teachers to government representatives and world leaders.

E-Net decided that for the Philippine campaign, the focus would be not only education for girl children – the overall theme of the Week of Action – but education for all children of vulnerable groups: children in poor, remote, and neglected communities; children in conflict-affected areas and war zones; children in Muslim and Indigenous People's communities; child workers; abused children; out-of-school youth; and children with special needs and different abilities.

While this decision was valid in the context of a campaigning activity which necessitated focusing on relevant themes, it reflects what has already been mentioned: because of the country's overall achievements in the education of girls, E-net may not be devoting to the latter the kind of attention that it still deserves. This is something that the network will have to address in the future, given the fact that gender inequalities still exist among certain groups, as discussed earlier.

Education For All: evolving partnerships between government and civil society

In the Philippines, the participation of CSOs during the EFA I assessment process, and in the consultations convened by the Department of Education immediately following the World Education Forum in Dakar in 2000, was a significant feature of the evolving relations between civil society and the government. There were constructive efforts to reach out and share views on matters related to EFA strategies, structure, and implementation. But the outcome in terms of policy reform, and in terms of developing a viable partnership between government and civil society, left much to be desired.

During the EFA assessment, NGOs raised important issues, citing poverty, war, and militarisation, the lack of democratic participation, corruption in government, and inadequate budget as factors affecting access to and quality of education. They also noted the problems of discrimination against girls, Muslim children, and differently abled children. These problems are manifested in gender biases in the school curricula and textbooks, in disparities in access – particularly in marginalised rural communities – and in the absence of education programmes catering especially to rural girls and disadvantaged children. Unfortunately, most of the issues raised during the EFA assessment were ignored and never included in the official report – a fact providing evidence of a partnership in which CSOs were not considered equal members, whose positions and contributions should be granted due attention.

More specifically the difficulties experienced by civil society during the first two years of EFA II can be attributed to the failure of attempts to convene the proposed 'grand alliance' of all stakeholders in the education sector. Having recognised that partnership was critical to the success of the EFA project, the Philippine government tried to set up a National Committee on Education For All (NCEFA), to bring together the various sectors and stakeholders concerned with education issues. These would have included the Department of Education, the National Economic and Development Authority, the Commission on Higher Education, the Commission on the Welfare of Children, the Technical Education Skills Development Authority, the Department of the Interior and Local Government, and the Department of Budget and Management.

However, the government did not pursue the plan to set up the NCEFA: the then Education Secretary dismissed the idea as 'just an additional layer of bureaucracy'. Instead, it relied on existing government structures which were not designed for inter-sectoral co-operation and were not conducive to partnership with civil society. In failing to pursue this plan, the government missed a good opportunity to mobilise and work with local communities, NGOs, parents, and other stakeholders in achieving EFA goals.

Thus, CSO–government engagement on post-Dakar processes lost momentum, largely because of the government's vacillation at a time when it should have been pursuing the EFA II planning process and defining the terms of partnership with CSOs. After a change in the leadership of the Department of Education in March 2001, following the change of government, the EFA planning process was put to one side and virtually halted for about two years. As a result, the Philippines was not able to meet the deadline of December 2002 for completing the EFA process. For the second time, the government failed to convene the NCEFA, which should have served as the organisational framework for bringing together stakeholders in the education sector. The draft Executive Order creating the NCEFA specified that a representative from civil society would co-chair the committee. Thus, the evolving partnership between the civil society and the government suffered a blow and did not mature into a more formal and institutionalised partnership with a well-defined structure and terms of engagement.

After two years, the Department of Education resumed the EFA planning, beginning in September 2002. However, instead of the proposed NCEFA, four Technical Working Groups (TWGs) were created: on Early Childhood Care and Development; on Formal Education; on Alternative Learning Systems; and on Governance and Financing. The TWGs would represent an inter-agency and multi-sectoral body with civil-society participation. In addition, unlike the proposed NCEFA, the working groups are designed to act as recommendatory bodies with still undefined parameters for civil-society participation. Thus an opportunity to create the preconditions for a viable and genuine partnership has again been missed.

New opportunities for such a partnership developed again when E-Net was asked by the Department of Education to represent civil society in the four TWGs. In March 2003, a Visioning Workshop on the EFA was convened in preparation for the drafting of the EFA Plan 2015. E-Net actively participated in the workshop, bringing along its reform agenda for consideration in formulating the EFA plans. Although differences in perspective and priorities between the government and the network became apparent, the two parties shared common views in many areas, including appreciation of critical gaps in access to basic education and the need to mainstream alternative learning systems.

For its part, the Department of Education participated by sending key officers to speak in forums organised by E-Net during the Global Campaign Week of Action in April 2003, the theme of which was girls' education and vulnerable children. E-Net began to lay the groundwork for a more productive partnership with government and other stakeholders to address these critical issues. Later that year, E-Net participated in a multi-sectoral meeting called by the Department of Education, as part of the planning exercise, this time to validate identified strategies for successful Plan realisation. E-net acknowledged the opening of spaces for civil-society involvement in the processes, but pushed for full participation in all the phases, beyond the Plan formulation. It seemed that the Department of Education was being selective when determining which specific processes were open and which were not. For instance, E-Net was not invited to the important Second National Workshop on EFA 2015, where programme interventions were developed and strategies mapped out.

The validation meeting that followed opened up space for E-Net to comment and give recommendations on the country targets, interventions, and strategies. These emphasised a special focus on affirmative actions to address critical gaps in education for the marginalised, excluded, and vulnerable (MEV) groups, and the creation of a gender-fair education policy. Crucially, E-Net called for strengthened partnerships between government agencies and civil society.

CSOs have long engaged with the government on various education policies and programmes. Earlier, such engagements tended to be confrontational, but spaces have begun to open up for genuine participation by civil society. Partnerships between E-Net members and government were also forged for specific projects, such as those on early childhood care and development (with Community of Learners Foundation, Narito Munting Puso Club, PLAN Philippines, and PINSAMA) and non-formal education and alternative learning systems (with Education for Life Foundation, Popular Education for People's Empowerment, and Trainers' Collective, among others). A recent success in policy change, the result of lobbying by Environment Science for Social Change, was the issuing of an Executive Order officially recognising schools for indigenous people. There was also joint advocacy, with Oxfam, on the educational needs of children in especially difficult circumstances, particularly the Muslim children in conflict-torn areas in Mindanao, southern Philippines. Together with the ILO and *barangay* (village) councils, the Alliance of Concerned Teachers succeeded in mobilising various sectors of the community to reduce the number of girls working as street vendors, and the number of boys employed to push passenger trolleys along the railroad tracks; they were supported to return to school if they had left it, or focus on studying if they had been juggling school and work at the same time.

Education For All: lessons learned from the partnership process

In summary, engagement between government and civil society on Education For All has been characterised by the proactive stance of CSOs working on education and related concerns. Such initiatives have helped to define and stretch the extent of the engagement. The presence of reform-oriented people in government, who were open to new ideas, also facilitated co-operation on EFA processes.

There are evident differences between the framework and approaches of CSOs and those of the government. NGOs tend to emphasise the importance of transparency, participation, innovation, quality, and relevance. They question what they perceive to be the elitist orientation of the education system, and they advocate thorough reforms of the education sector. The government, on the other hand, manifests a preference for more traditional approaches. While the education bureaucracy professes openness to stakeholders' participation, the education-sector bureaucracy tends to cling to the traditional idea that education is the sole business of government. Thus, it usually takes tremendous effort on the part of government, especially at the local level, to adjust to concepts of partnerships and joint ventures with civil society, which includes NGOs, local communities, teachers, parents, and students. It has often been easier for them to relate to private sector entities such as businesses.

At the same time, a partnership has been emerging. In reviewing the engagement that took place around the EFA project, E-Net members identified several factors that helped to create a favourable environment for co-operation between government and civil society:

- NGOs' dynamism and willingness to work together on education issues.
- Their continuous tracking of policy development, which has kept the network informed of the opportunities for engagement with government.
- Cultivating effective and strategic contacts within the Department of Education, particularly with individuals who expressed openness to the network's reform agenda.
- Participation in national and international conferences, dialogues, and forums attended by representatives of both government and civil society.
- Actively exploring and promoting practical proposals to government officials concerning the role of CSOs in the EFA structure and processes.

- Continuous networking with UN agencies, international organisations, and NGOs in other countries, and participation in international campaigns on education-related issues.
- Engaging the government in national, local, regional, and international arenas to broaden the platform for engagement and to gain recognition as serious stakeholders in the education sector.
- A clear advocacy plan to ensure continuing engagement.

There are also lessons to be learned on partnerships among civil-society organisations themselves. The formation and existence of E-Net is a test case for civil-society partnership on the EFA, and by implication also for partnerships working on girls' education. As such, its experiences will identify the elements that make for positive synergies among CSOs working on a common agenda.

The first lesson concerns the importance of the role played by a small group of key individuals. The network is a very broad alliance of diverse groups. Before it could develop formal structures, it was a core of active men and women who sustained engagements and provided vision and direction. A core group of committed and informed people remains a crucial feature of the network, though with the addition of new individuals.

Secondly, although a structure was put in place by the General Assembly, the network did not adhere to it strictly, but retained flexibility in its working arrangements. For instance, rather than adopting a bureaucratic system for reaching consensus, it encouraged its members to discuss positions and concerns in an open manner. When appropriate, members of the Board, the Executive Committee, and the National Secretariat joined experts in specific fields to negotiate position papers and comment on government plans.

Thirdly, E-Net adopted a two-pronged approach in the EFA planning and implementation process. It engaged the government at the national level within the proposed NCEFA, and it also initiated the formation of local committees at the ground level (LCEFA). The initiative intends to achieve several objectives. First, the LCEFA allows the active participation of local members and chapters at the local level. Second, it affords E-Net additional flexibility to pursue its advocacy initiatives. Third, the LCEFA provides another platform for engaging the government on EFA-related processes.

Currently, emerging forms of partnerships are dictated by the nature of the coalitions that have come together as local core groups for EFA. While some have opted to become formal E-Net chapters, others have chosen to remain distinct, integrating the EFA framework in their existing programmes.

Efforts at the national level were not abandoned, however, and recently E-Net was designated as the co-chair (with the government's Department of

Education) of a nationwide alliance, intended to be the driving force of a popular movement to achieve education for all.

Finally, links with the regional and international actors in the EFA campaign enabled the national coalition to participate in venues where government actors were also present. This gave additional credibility to the CSOs involved, so that initial discussions of issues at the international level could subsequently be pursued locally with government officials.

Cultural bias against girls' education

The Philippines has earned the distinction of being one of the few developing countries where there is basic parity between boys and girls in school access, retention, and achievement. The EFA Assessment Report went so far as to note that in the Philippines, the real problem is getting boys to enrol – and remain – in school. Education indicators reveal that girls have consistently out-performed their male counterparts in gross and net primary enrolment rates, cohort survival to grade 6, repetition and dropout rates, and learning achievement. The superior performance of female children was observed in almost all years from 1990 to 1999, and it applies generally to both rural and urban areas. This led government planners to declare that gender parity is no longer a relevant target in its EFA programming.

Philippine NGOs, including E-Net, agree with the claim that there is gender parity in education – when it is assessed in terms of key performance indicators. E-Net acknowledges this as a significant achievement, worth studying and replicating in other countries. Because of this, the network intends to continue to act in partnership with the government and other organisations to ensure that the achievement is sustained.

All the same, E-Net remains committed to retaining a gender dimension in its overall education-reform agenda. This is because in the Philippines, gender biases are still deeply rooted in the school system. These are manifested not only in gender stereotyping in textbooks, but also in school policies and practices and in curricula. The school climate discriminates against women and girls and creates conditions which engender violence and sexual harassment, especially against girl children. The practice of expelling teenage schoolgirls who become pregnant is still prevalent.

E-Net further notes that social barriers which prevent girls from attending and staying in schools are especially evident among disadvantaged groups, particularly those who suffer discrimination on the basis of their ethnicity, religion, language, economic class, or disability. Among these groups, girls are more likely to be withdrawn from school than boys, for example to take up domestic responsibilities when the family is large or the mother takes employment in the city or overseas. Distance from school also discourages girls from attending, especially when they reach the age of puberty. Furthermore, girls and young women predominate in certain categories of child worker: domestic helpers, unpaid family workers, and those forced into prostitution. NGOs working in poor and high-conflict areas and among indigenous peoples note the lower participation and high dropout rate among female children.

 On the basis of this understanding, E-Net sees a number of measures as essential for strengthening its own work on gender and girls' education, and that of its individual members. First of all, it recognises its own limited understanding and knowledge of many aspects of gender disparities in education. Since robust data and reliable analysis are essential to effective advocacy, it advocates disaggregation of all data, to monitor the performance of girl children and especially those from vulnerable and disadvantaged backgrounds.

In addition, E-net believes that the various sectoral networks may share a degree of complacency with regard to achievements in girls' education. It thus should encourage coalitions and networks to come together to promote the achievement of internationally agreed targets. A first step would be that of sharing agendas. For example, E-Net could take on the priorities of the NGO Coalition on the Convention on the Rights of Children (CRC) through a rights-based education framework approach. The NGO-CRC, on the other hand, could integrate the EFA frame in its interventions. An advocacy plan specially designed for the education rights of the girl-child could be designed as a focal joint undertaking.

In addition E-net recognises that the promotion of girls' education needs to occur at all levels, not only nationally. In terms of the gender-related content of curriculum and education materials, much of the engagement must take place at the national level. In terms of policies and practices concerning the learning environment, advocacy should aim to change prevailing attitudes and beliefs, but it should also target local education structures, since the 2003 Decentralization of Governance in Basic Education Law has invested considerable authority in them.

Conclusion

At a meeting held during the World Education Forum (WEF) in 2003, UNESCO Director General Koichiro Matsura issued a document entitled 'Synthesis Report: Involvement of Civil Society in EFA'. This report validates the approach of E-Net's plans in the following statement:

> *The role of civil society in community-based governance bears relevance for the other four dimensions of civil society's involvement: alternative service provider, innovator, informed critic and advocate, and policy partner.*

Civil-society groups face tremendous challenges in pursuing their reform agenda. They must develop their capabilities and mechanisms for engagement to maximise their participation in the national, local, and global spheres. Engaging government on the EFA project will be a long struggle for genuine and strategic partnership. At the same time, CSOs still need to maintain their independence and pursue their own initiatives. They should agree common platforms and continue to engage and partner with government where there are unities and synergy. Strengthened international partnerships can help to bring pressure on governments to open up such avenues for civil-society participation.

Gender equity in all aspects of education by 2005 must become and remain an explicit priority of all such partnerships, especially to ensure that the impressive gains made in girls' education in the Philippines become a reality among those groups that still experience multiple forms of marginalisation and neglect in education. The nature and quality of partnerships forged with government and among civil-society groups will be one of the conditions defining the chances of achieving gender parity and quality Education For All, preferably sooner than 2015.

Rene R. Raya is a member of the Management Collective of Action for Economic Reforms (AER), a policy study and advocacy group which focuses on financial, trade, governance, and human-development issues. He represents AER in the Education Network (E-Net) and co-ordinates the Task Force on Education Financing. He is also co-convenor of Social Watch Philippines, an international network of citizens' groups which monitors the progress of countries in poverty eradication, human development, and social and gender equity.

Raquel de Guzman-Castillo is the National Co-ordinator for the Civil Society Network for Education Reforms. E-Net, as it is more widely known, comprises more than 120 members and affiliates nationwide in the Philippines, and is a platform for education-related initiatives, partnerships, and advocacy for life-long, good-quality education for all.

5 Complementary provision: State and society in Bangladesh

Ahmadullah Mia

Bangladesh has made great strides in the movement for universal basic education, particularly girls' education, since the world conference on Education For All (EFA), held in Jomtien, Thailand, in 1990. Gross enrolment rates at primary level have reached 97 per cent for both girls and boys – up from 81 per cent for boys and 70 per cent for girls in 1991. At the secondary level, the level of girls' enrolment has surpassed that of boys.

How has this transformation taken place? While high-level commitment and leadership have been crucial, in practice the improvement is the result of a range of diverse partnerships between the government and civil-society groups, educationists, researchers, and donors. This chapter examines the nature of partnerships between the government and civil-society actors, mainly NGOs, in the specific context of girls' education. Using a range of case studies, it seeks to analyse not only the different types of partnership that exist, but also the basic principles that lie behind successful partnerships. It focuses on the establishment of complementary roles between State institutions and NGOs, and the mutual acceptance of each other's roles as valuable and necessary.

Bangladesh ranks low (140th among 174 countries) in the UNDP's gender-related development index (GDI).[1] While the government and civil society have reiterated their commitment to women's advancement and acknowledged the role of education in this process, in line with global commitments such as the Beijing Platform for Action, the International Conference on Population and Development at Cairo, the Education For All movement, and the Millennium Development Goals (MDGs), the emphasis on the role of partnerships in this process has been more recent.

Both the Jomtien conference and the Dakar Framework for Action (2000) articulated the importance of participation for achieving the goals of Education For All. While governments were responsible for ensuring that provision was adequate to meet the goals, the importance of civil society's participation in planning, implementation, and monitoring was seen as crucial if indeed Education For All was to be acknowledged as a 'movement' and as 'everybody's business'. The principle of participation came to be one of the values that the government, civil-society groups, and the external support providers wanted to uphold.

Education for women and girls: government commitments to partnership

Bangladesh has shown its strong commitment to prioritising education, and particularly girls' education. The government has taken several important policy decisions since the 1980s to encourage girls to enter higher education, to reduce gender disparity in education and employment, and to promote the empowerment of women[2] (Mia and Khan 2003). Among them were specific measures to increase school access for girls and reduce illiteracy among adult women.

The promulgation of the Compulsory Primary Education Act 1990 was a bold legal step. A second crucial step was the introduction of the incentive programme at both primary and secondary levels of education. This programme, known as *Food for Education*, came into operation in the early 1990s. It has been recently reformed to offer cash stipends to poor children at the primary level, and exemption from payment of tuition fees for girls in rural secondary schools. The programme's intent was to attract girls into government schools and registered non-government schools (and retain them, once enrolled), and thus attain gender parity in schooling. The Prime Minister of the present government has announced an extension of incentive programmes to include girl students at higher-secondary level.

In 1992, the Prime Minister launched the National Campaign on Social Mobilization for Basic Education, underscoring the importance of education for girls. The campaign had a high profile, with a great deal of media publicity, including a series of animated films entitled *Meena*, which highlighted the importance of girls' education in the day-to-day life of poor families. As a part of the SAARC[3] development co-operation agenda, the Ministry of Women's Affairs formulated the Decade Action Plan for the Girl Child 1991–2001 and launched this plan with the title *Samata* (meaning 'equality') in 1993. The salient aspects of the plan included strategies and interventions to facilitate girls' access to basic/primary and secondary education, and incentives for girls' education. With the launching of *Samata*, NGOs already active in the field, especially those supported by regional and international bodies, found themselves working in an encouraging environment, as their role was perceived to complement the government programmes.

The contribution of NGOs to education, particularly non-formal education (NFE),[4] was more widely recognised in the 1990s, following the World Conference on Education For All, held at Jomtien (WCEFA, 1990). The government of Bangladesh found it convenient to increase its engagement in partnerships through special Integrated Non-formal Education Programmes (INFEP, 1991). Subsequently, with the establishment of the Directorate of Non-formal Education (DNFE) under the Prime Minister's secretariat, non-formal education was accorded a higher priority. A special emphasis was placed on promoting women's literacy and girls' education in the NFE programmes.[5]

Partnership between the government and civil society (NGOs), though still restricted to NFE (the formal sector continuing to be viewed as essentially a State sector), was strengthened in 1991 with the setting up of the Campaign for Education (CAMPE). The membership of this coalition of NGOs engaged in education programmmes in Bangladesh now numbers more than 425. Apart from being a network and a link between the grassroots and policy levels, CAMPE as an advocacy agency has ensured that the voices of NGOs are not completely ignored by the State and that some semblance of partnership is maintained by providing space for NGOs in decision-making processes, and not treating them as mere implementers of State policies. To maintain an independent status, CAMPE and some of its member NGOs have undertaken a wide range of activities, including research; the compilation, documentation, and dissemination of information; educational projects focused on women and girls; comprehensive, gender-sensitive community development; seminars, conferences, and round-table discussions; memoranda addressed to policy makers and decision makers; rallies; lobby meetings; and media campaigns. One such project, entitled 'Education Watch', has had a strong influence on government policy.

Some examples of partnership

Following WCEFA, debates about partnership in the field of education focused on 'education for all' rather than on gender equality. The Child Rights Convention, which preceded WCEFA, also emphasised the rights of all children. Yet, given the reality of girls' disadvantage in all spheres of life and in all social spaces (family, community, school, and work), it has been recognised that, without special attention to girls' situation, parity cannot be achieved, nor can the rights of all children be realised.

NGOs have in this regard argued the needs for a girl-friendly school environment, increased numbers of female teachers, increased training facilities for female teachers, improved physical conditions in schools (with facilities such as separate toilets for girls), and reviews of curriculum and teaching/learning materials to eliminate gender bias or stereotyping. Lobbyists have also urged the need to support poor families to earn higher incomes, which would have a positive influence on parents' attitudes to girls' education.

Some NGOs, such as BRAC (Bangladesh Rural Advancement Committee), Dhaka Ahsania Mission (DAM), the Underprivileged Children's Education Programme (UCEP), and Centre for Mass Education in Science (CMES),[6] provide opportunities for primary- and secondary-level education within the framework of their own programmes. These contain features sensitive to the special needs of girls at school.[7] Some of these programmes are discussed in some detail below, to enable an analysis of their strengths and weaknesses in terms of working in partnership with the State and other actors.

Bangladesh Rural Advancement Committee (BRAC)

BRAC has engaged in direct partnership with the government under an agreement to run several hundred community schools in the country – schools which had not been properly functional earlier. By 2002, BRAC had 44 community schools offering primary education, 27 of which were offering the full range of primary education from grade 1 to grade 5. The main problem has been the government's reluctance to pay recurrent costs, despite its wish that the schools should operate according to government standards and regulations. This problem is discouraging other NGOs from running primary schools.

BRAC has derived its strength from its track record in running educational programmes, particularly in non-formal basic/primary education, since the 1980s. Its organisational strength and its capacity in developing teaching materials with a suitable curriculum have put it in a strong position to negotiate with the government bureaucracy. BRAC's innovations in NFE in particular have been well accepted by both the government and the NGO community. BRAC has set up a special unit called GOB Partnership Unit (GPU) with the objective 'to strengthen the national primary education system'. One important new initiative was the establishment of Chandina Learning Improvement Project (CLIP), to demonstrate the potential for raising standards in all grades by using experimental supplementary materials and new teaching methodologies.

Other BRAC–GOB joint programmes include adult education through literacy centres (in collaboration with DNFE), and (in collaboration with DNFE and UNICEF) schools for 'hard to reach children', between the ages of 8 and 14 years, working in hazardous occupations. Many other NGOs also partner the government in implementing these two programmes, but BRAC's large-scale involvement has given it the ability to negotiate the provision of supplementary material along with that supplied by the DNFE. The major problem experienced in running this programme jointly with the government was that the curriculum and the teaching materials provided by DNFE were not adequate or suitable to the learning needs of the target group, yet their use was compulsory.

One major objective of the GPU was to enhance the efficiency of the government primary schools by offering pedagogical training to teachers. The government has been slow to respond to this suggestion. However, BRAC has taken the initiative and now runs 1,273 low-cost pre-primary schools, promoting them to the government as a means of improving performance in the primary-education system. In 2002, 36,469 children, of whom 59 per cent were girls, were enrolled in BRAC's pre-primary schools. BRAC has also established its own teacher-training programmes.

It appears from the above that in overall terms BRAC has been engaged in a close working partnership with the government. The strength of the BRAC–GOB partnership lay in BRAC's attempt to complement the government's efforts by running a 'quality-driven programme' which sought to 'build and share knowledge of new and more cost-effective ways of delivering primary education'.[8] The general support that all NGOs receive from the government is official approval to receive external donor funding for implementing their programmes, provided that they (NGOs) are registered with the NGO Affairs Bureau (a government body) and fulfil other government regulations. The only exception is the implementation of NFE projects by NGOs under contractual agreements with the government. What seems to be essential in this case is BRAC's investment in creating a unit – the GPU – at the national level, to negotiate with the government on all matters, as and when they arise. It is perhaps the only NGO that has been able to enter the domain of formal education and negotiate some flexibility in curriculum, textbooks, and pedagogical practices. Most other NGOs, lacking such capacity, either work independently or remain in an unequal partnership – implementing programmes as contractors for the government, rather than being able to contribute to agenda setting or even influencing State planning and implementation.

Centre for Mass Education in Science (CMES)

A case in point is the Centre for Mass Education in Science (CMES), which offers a good model of innovative NFE intervention, with sensitivity to girls' needs in the context of rural poverty. CMES participated in the NFE programme (NFE Projects I and II) of DNFE. Like other NGOs, the organisation found it difficult to work with the government system, owing to the policy of standardising costs and materials irrespective of contextual differences. In the area where CMES was assigned to work, it did not have the freedom to recruit staff required by the nature of the programme. The local government staff wanted to have their own people recruited; CMES could not agree to this, and its contract was terminated as a result.

Dhaka Ahsania Mission (DAM) and the Ganokendra programme

The Dhaka Ahsania Mission (DAM), while maintaining links with the government at the centre, has tried therefore to establish negotiating strength in its dealing with local government bodies. Over several years of working at the village community level, it has evolved an innovative model of Community Learning Centres, known locally as *Ganokendra*, to provide and facilitate basic education, life skills, and some vocational skills. This is a multi-functional community-based institution aiming to empower poor people. The provision of rural need-based services through *Ganokendra* encourages the development of a learning culture and eventually a knowledge-based society, the rural community being involved in the process and taking the benefit. Nearly 800 'Ganokendras', spread over several regions of the country, are now addressing rural poverty through non-formal education.

The *Ganokendra* process of working involves the broad-based participation of local people and government service-delivery agencies at the local level in the fields of education, health and family planning, women's development, youth development, social services, agriculture, public health (water and sanitation), livestock, fisheries, and forestry. In addition, *Ganokendra* draws on the participation of the Union Parishad (the lowest tier of the local self-government structure) in organising local development activities. The Parishad now makes use of the *Ganokendra* in implementing several activities, including immunisation and marriage registration.

It is to be noted here that research and programme-review reports consistently indicate the alarming inefficiency of primary schools administered or supported by the government. In comparison, non-formal education through NGOs appears to produce better results in terms of literacy.[9] Some weaknesses in the public schooling system are its bureaucratic and centralised management, lack of authority and resources at the local level, and lack of a sense of ownership of the school on the part of parents and the local community. On the other hand, non-formal education provided by NGOs seems to give better results, as it works under flexible arrangements, with close involvement of parents. The multi-functional character of the *Ganokendras*, in particular, tends to help poor families to access educational facilities (NFE or formal primary schooling), and it creates some interest in the Union Parishad in efforts to eradicate illiteracy from the locality. However, the change of chairperson and members of the

Union Parishad, after elections every five years, can affect the level of co-operation of the Parishad. Similar is the case with relevant government staff in various departments at the local level. A key element in effective partnership seems to be a shared vision and mission, and the willingness of individuals to compromise in order to achieve this – which is often difficult when people suddenly find themselves in positions of power in government, whether elected or appointed, often for a short period of time.

Notable among other difficulties experienced by DAM are that *Ganokendras* do not all function at the same level. The strength of these local-level centres varies between geographic areas, in accordance with the variation in economic and social conditions, and in the attitudes of local government bodies. Similarly the management capacity of the local people is not always at the level necessary to give long-term institutional sustainability to the *Ganokendra*.

In recognition of the potential value of the *Ganokendra* model, however, it is now being implemented in the urban areas at both primary and secondary levels of education. Special emphasis is laid on education of girls from poor and disadvantaged families, encouraging them to move on to DAM's Vocational Training Institute in order to enhance their chances of upward economic and social mobility. Transport is provided for poor/disadvantaged girls (and boys) to enable them to take advantage of vocational training. While the *Ganokendra* focuses on girls and women in all its activities, 25 per cent of the organisational membership consists of men; this is a conscious strategy to make the *Ganokendra* an effective local institution. However, it has been noted that male members are often over-represented in the management of the *Ganokendra*.

Underprivileged Children's Education Programme (UCEP)

A final example of partnership, focusing on the realm of work and on developing a partnership between NGOs and the private sector, is the Underprivileged Children's Education Programme (UCEP). It offers an integrated pattern of education and technical/vocational training, especially addressed to poor working children in urban contexts. Stressing a rights-based approach, UCEP attempts to ensure gender balance; organises training in trades most suitable to the economic and cultural context; and facilitates girls' access to training by providing stipends and transport to and from the training centres. Spread over four metropolitan cities, UCEP runs 30 general schools, three technical training centres, and three para-vocational training centres. In the July–December session of 2002, total participants in general education were 10,929 girls and 10,288 boys; in the technical training and para-vocational training centres there was a total of 800 girls and 1,221 boys. By the time UCEP participants complete technical training, they have reached at least 15 years of age and are eligible to enter the labour market. UCEP follows the curriculum of public primary schools, but adapts to the special needs of the poor children and applies the flexibility of the non-formal system, giving pupils a choice of morning and afternoon shifts – a system which allows them to learn while they earn.

UCEP has proved that poverty does not inevitably entail the sacrifice of education, and also that poor parents can be motivated to educate their children, even girls, when education is perceived to be meaningful for real life, especially for earning an income. It has two levels of students' graduation, primary and lower-secondary levels, respectively grade 5 and grade 8 of the public school system. After grade 5, students can choose to take para-vocational training; after grade 8 they can choose technical-vocational training. The graduates of the latter are eligible to take the test for national skills standard III (NSS III) under the National Technical Education Board. On account of the accreditation of its training, the UCEP technical graduates are accorded preference in the formal employment market.

UCEP has a policy of employing a higher than usual proportion of female teachers, to encourage participation of girls in both general and technical education. Its partnership with private-sector industries, business, and services to promote employment of trained girls is developed in ways that are both structured and unstructured. It is promoted through the 'Employment and Field Services' component of UCEP, in which employment counselling is provided to the graduates, and contact is maintained with the prospective employers, to arrange practical work experience, regular employment, and on-the-job training. In 2002–2003, 94 per cent of the technical graduates obtained employment through UCEP.[10]

In spite of its reputation as a model for transforming disadvantaged children and adolescents into productive human beings through education and training, UCEP has had difficulties in scaling up its work. Levels of motivation among employers are low, there is a shortage of employment opportunities, and trade unions active in public-sector enterprises are unsympathetic. The greatest problem is the fact that UCEP's programme is more expensive than the conventional skills training provided either by government institutions or by other NGOs. Ensuring the high-quality skills demanded by employers requires higher investment. UCEP tries to cover costs by inviting co-operation from the employers and also by encouraging the trainees to share some of the costs, but fund-raising is not easy.

This case raises the very interesting issue of how to deliver education cheaply, particularly to the poor, and the problems of sustaining such an approach. Quality requires resources. The government gives no financial support to UCEP, nor does it show an interest in replicating the model. The reason is stated to be the higher costs involved, but perhaps the real reason is the rigidity of the public education sector, and the reluctance of officials and staff to accept new ideas. The government-funded technical training centres do not produce good-quality graduates, because they are poorly managed. Under the present circumstances, UCEP is heavily dependent on the support of donors, and as such its long-term sustainability is uncertain, despite widespread recognition of its valuable innovations. The general education provided by UCEP is not supported by the government either, as it cannot meet the conditions of the public sector, its prime consideration being to ensure that its systems are suitable and adaptable to the conditions of poor working boys and girls.

At the local level, through negotiations with city authorities or philanthropic individuals, UCEP has been able to establish a number of schools on donated land. This has been made possible by dint of the merits of its programmes. Once again an important lesson can be drawn from this experience: community participation is forthcoming for something that is perceived as being both useful and meaningful. But the impossibility of reducing poverty and providing employable skills of good quality without adequate investment is undeniable.

Tensions and difficulties in partnerships

As indicated above, in Bangladesh two major factors have influenced the partnership between the State and civil society, particularly NGOs, engaged in promoting education for all. One is that the contribution made by civil society is considered useful by the government, as well as by the donor partners supporting education programmes. Secondly, the WCEFA and the follow-up declaration in Dakar made a strong case for the participation of all concerned, and especially NGOs, in planning, implementing, and monitoring activities at the national level to achieve the EFA objectives within a set timetable. Thus the relationship between the government and the NGOs was expected to be founded on complementary roles and on mutual acceptance of these roles.

The mutuality between the parties was generally understood in the open dialogue. But in reality the government used the leverage of its bureaucratic authority to influence the NGOs, not always in a very positive way. Mutual mistrust and allegation, manifest or latent, has strained the relationship at times. The government considers the NGOs privileged by external donor support, but lacking in transparency and accountability. It is true that many NGO staff have developed an enviable life-style, thanks to funds from donors, which may offset the efficiency that they claim or the benefit that they make available to the target group; but it would be unfair to make this generalisation about the sector as a whole, especially the field-level staff, who often work for low pay and in difficult circumstances.

In their negotiations with the State, one of the major constraints faced by NGOs working primarily with disadvantaged groups is their need for financial support. They do not find it easy to make their programmes self-sustaining, especially when they offer services like technical-vocational education, which is expensive. The principles of cost recovery from the beneficiaries (as attempted by UCEP, DAM, and CMES) and cost reduction with support from the private sector (attempted by UCEP only) are helpful to some extent, but they are not enough and in most situations they are feasible. This makes the NGOs dependent on donor support or on the acceptance of unfavourable contracts from the government.

Secondly, a large number of NGOs offer primary-level education programmes that are shorter than those of the public education system: they last three or four years, instead of five. They do this by means of flexible school timetables, and they exercise better time management in the interest of their beneficiaries. Some use the public education curriculum, but in a condensed form, and they include additional contents more closely relevant to the realities of students' lives. This non-formal primary education is however not officially recognised as primary education by the government. The government wants NGOs and private bodies to establish primary schools based on government prescriptions; but these are not acceptable to NGOs, because they would entail loss of flexibility (in content and timing), which is one of the major strengths of their programmes.

It is for this reason, perhaps, that NGOs' work has been better acknowledged in their literacy programmes for adults than at the level of primary education. Government statistics on primary education do not show the performance of NGOs. By and large, NGO NFE programmes remain outside the purview of government, except for the public-sector programme in which NGOs were implementing agencies. Some reviews of these NFE programmes indicate that the government set rigid conditions, made unilateral decisions without discussion with the concerned NGOs, and in general treated the partner NGOs as contractors. And if the NGOs disagreed with these conditions, the partnership broke down – as in the case of the Centre for Mass Education in Science.

Further, the official NFE projects (four projects addressing different age groups, one of them specifically for hard-to-reach urban children) were very short-lived (nine months only). Given the short duration, limited and irregular financing, and rigid bureaucratic formalities imposed by the government, the NGO partners operated by temporarily employing low-quality teachers at unattractive salaries. They rented houses to run the centres for a short period, where facilities were poor and little care was taken to ensure good learning outcomes. The centres were closed within the given time limit of the project, before the learners could gain sustainable literacy. Available reports suggest that the selection of participants in the learning centres was not done carefully, nor was the assessment of learning outcomes done properly. Many of the programmes were run by NGOs which had no continuing commitment or long-standing expertise; some took whatever money was available, in a bid to survive and demonstrate their existence, with a view to future involvement. As a result, quality of performance was not satisfactory;[11] but rather than recognising the real issues, the poor performance was attributed to weak monitoring and supervision on the part of the government machinery. A few large national NGOs, such as BRAC, had substantial programme packages of their own, of which the government-supported NFE was only a small part, so they could overcome the difficulties by drawing upon their own strength, in addition to doing some hard bargaining with the government. But for the smaller NGOs the partnership with the government was more like a patron–client relationship: the NGOs were expected to accept whatever was given to them.

While the government considers NGOs to be lacking in accountability, the NGOs are critical of the government's tendency to use its bureaucratic system to regulate and control rather than facilitate, support, and promote the capacity of NGOs. It is alleged that in the selection of NGO partners for implementing NFE programmes, objectivity was not maintained, and instead rigid attitudes and corrupt practices prevailed on the part of some government officials. Government programmes tend to concentrate on quantitative targets and compromise on quality. Some programmes – for example, the Total Literacy Movement (TLM) – implemented under government supervision have been seriously criticised for wasting money. But the government claims that TLM has contributed to the eradication of illiteracy, despite some wastage of resources in the management process.

On the whole, it may not be unfair to say that there are continuing tensions between the government and NGOs. Lack of mutual trust and respect appears to strain relations. The government likes to issue circulars, rules of actions, codes of conduct, or instruments to regulate activities of NGOs and establish discipline (which is an expression of its unhappiness about the voluntary sector). In the process sometimes the two sides sit around a discussion table, at the initiative of either party, to share their views; but the final decision always remains in the hands of the government, and the NGO Affairs Bureau implements the administrative and policy regulations of the central administration.

It is usually the government that publishes national statistics. These are not undisputed, and independent studies tend to produce different data. NGOs commission independent studies or prepare separate review reports. The difference between the official reports and the NGO reports becomes unpalatable to both parties. Lack of trust persists.

Finally, the political climate determines the quality of partnerships. Conflict between the ruling party and NGO leaders has become an issue in recent years, with the State frowning on any sort of educational work aimed at increasing political awareness. It has been alleged that some NGO leaders have openly adopted political roles and mobilised the beneficiaries in favour of one political regime and against another. This has provoked annoyance and sharp scrutiny of NGOs suspected of playing a political role. These circumstances create division among members of the NGO community itself, as happened with the recent creation of a new apex (co-ordinating) body of NGOs, in opposition to the earlier one. It is clear that NGOs are not a uniform group: they differ greatly in size, capacity, quality, ideology, and negotiating strength.

Opportunities for partnership remain

Despite the tensions described above, neither the government nor the NGOs have ever denied the necessity of partnership between them. The government has sought the involvement of NGOs in various projects which required nationwide personnel and logistical support that the government could not provide in the short term. Besides, with their independent community-based programmes, NGOs generate resources or bring them into the community, mobilise people, and provide services to fill the gaps left by the normal delivery system of the government. They supplement official services, reaching out to sections of the society, and difficult geographic locations, where the government delivery system is inadequate.

NGOs have been accepted at the grassroots as useful social entities. Historical reality shows them having roots in the national movement for reconstruction. They have an edge in terms of experimenting, innovating, and finding additional resources. They have received recognition from the external world. Other groups in civil society can take advantage of the presence of NGOs in playing a pro-active role in social mobilisation for change in the society, and so does the government. Most NGOs would feel gratified to take part in government projects, for the sake of establishing their identity as well as their credibility in the community where they work. For all these reasons, both parties consider that their roles complement each other.

The EFA initiatives brought the two parties closer in practical terms. Achieving the EFA goals and working on the National Plan of Action, with increased participation of the community, has created an absolute necessity for maintaining a working relationship between the government and the NGOs. The latter have links with people of all social strata, in all occupations, organising discussion/opinion forums, seeking to make their voices heard by the government decision makers. Indeed, to maintain the momentum of progress towards the creation of a 'learning society', and to promote new and pragmatic ways of involving the masses, NGOs can make a vital contribution.

It is understood that in power relations and decision-making processes, relations between the government and the NGOs will continue to be unbalanced, the former being in the advantageous position. However, opportunities will continue to exist for the NGOs to participate in the national programmes, so long as their credibility is not lost and they do not present themselves as acting in their own vested interests. In spite of difficult times now and then, CAMPE and some NGOs and civil-society research groups have been able to sit around the discussion table, negotiate, engage in dialogue, and even conduct lobbying without being confrontational. Such a working strategy must be pursued as a policy of the NGOs.

Both the Jomtien and Dakar declarations provided a framework for action. The government and civil society remain committed to them and to strengthening their efforts and enhancing their collaboration in all the processes of educational development for promoting literacy and education for girls and women. Both parties need to seize the opportunities and build more partnerships based on equality and mutual respect.

Ahmadullah Mia was Professor and Director of the Institute of Social Welfare and Research of the University of Dhaka from 1964 to 1992. He worked as the chief executive of the Underprivileged Children's Education Programme, providing basic education combined with vocational skills training.

Notes

1   World Bank: *Key Challenges for the Next Millennium*, April 1999.

2   Ahmadullah Mia and N. I. Khan: *Girls' Education: Bangladesh Country Study* (ASPBAE-GCE Joint Initiative), 2003.

3   South Asian Regional Co-operation, of which Bangladesh was the initiator and then a member.

4   NGOs, big and small all over the country, were the implementing partners of the Government NFE Projects, named NFE Project-I, Project-II, Project-III, and Project-IV. Currently two big government projects on post-literacy and continuing education for human development (PLCEHD) have involved NGOs as implementing partners. These projects are designed to implement education and vocational skills training together.

5   Civil-society partnership became very broadly based, particularly with the involvement of a number of apex bodies of NGOs and networks, besides more than 400 individual NGOs and other civil-society groups. While NGOs became implementing partners of NFE programme, their forums also played an active role in promoting the interests (especially education and

rights) of women and girls through dialogues, rallies, campaigns, research, publication, publicity, and lobbying. Apex bodies or networks include CAMPE, Nari Uddog (Women's Initiatives), UBINIG (Policy Research for Development Alternative), and BSAF (Bangladesh Child Rights Forum).

6   BRAC and DAM have Community Learning Centres; DAM, UCEP, and CMES have Technical-Vocational Training Schools/Centres in addition to general education.

7   They (and most other NGOs) set up schools in locations to ensure easy access for girls in terms of physical distance from home, employment of female teachers, and use of gender-sensitive curriculum and teaching-learning materials. At post-primary or secondary level, skills training is provided to increase the capacity of girls to earn an income, reduce dependency on other members of family, and exercise their rights in family and social situations. In these education and training programmes, adolescent girls' needs (such as basic orientation on family life and health/ reproductive health education) are addressed, in addition to vocational training for gainful work.

8   Education Programme (NFPE Phase III) April 1999–March 2004, BRAC Report 1998, p. 111.

9   Manzoor Ahmed, Samir R. Nath, and Kazi Saleh Ahmed: *Education Watch 2002: Literacy in Bangladesh*, Campaign for Popular Education, 2003.

10   Further details on UCEP education and technical–vocational skill training, and links with employment markets and private industries will be found in Ahmadulla Mia: *A Promising Path: Education, Skills Training and Employment*, Underprivileged Children's Educational Programmes (UCEP), 1995.

11   A recent review refers to a number of studies on NFE projects supported by the government NFE programme (Akbar and Mia: *Literacy, Basic and Continuing Education: Approaches and Contribution to Human Development*, Dhaka Ahsania Mission, 2003).

6 Partnerships from below: indigenous rights and girls' education in the Peruvian Amazon

Sheila Aikman

This chapter considers partnership from the perspective of an indigenous organisation in the south-eastern Peruvian Amazon, the Federation of Natives of Madre de Dios – FENAMAD.[1] This inter-ethnic federation, representing the indigenous peoples of the region, was established in 1982 at a time when their rights and interests were under intensifying threat. The chapter investigates 'partnership' through the lens of the Federation's work for the recognition of local communities' rights to be consulted in the matter of their children's schooling. This process led them into new relations with other indigenous and non-indigenous organisations and networks, as well as with institutionalised education in the control of State and Church.

The chapter charts the educational history of 'Magda', an indigenous girl from a FENAMAD base community, and her experience of formal education controlled by State and Church. From 1983 to the late 1990s she was a full-time student, and today she is the only person from her village to have graduated as a qualified primary-school teacher. Through her story we glimpse the gendered education that she has received, and we consider why she is seen to lack the skills and insights that would make her a valuable resource for the kind of education that the Federation wants to promote today.

The sections of the chapter follow the various levels of Magda's education – primary, secondary, and teacher training – which also represent major phases in the development of the Federation and its alliances.

Partnerships and the indigenous movement

The term 'partnership' is used extensively inn the field of international development today, but the types of relationship that it denotes can vary enormously. Partnerships with local organisations may be used by donors or large NGOs as a panacea for the shortcomings of development co-operation; they are often regarded as a means of ensuring greater cost-effectiveness, or relevance and credibility. The use of the term reflects a conceptual move from 'beneficiary' to 'stakeholder', and a development of strategies to engage citizens more directly in establishing and negotiating priorities for policy and for holding governments accountable. It may also denote a process of building local ownership of development initiatives, or building capacities so that partners can do things for themselves on the basis of locally defined development strategies (Hauck and Land 2000). The OECD talks of participatory development as

> *standing for a partnership which is built upon a basis of a dialogue among various actors (stakeholders) during which the agenda is set jointly and local views and indigenous knowledge are deliberately sought and respected.*
> (OECD 1994, cited in Cornwall 2000)

However, as certain critics have pointed out, this position is very idealised, and the actual implementation of such a notion of partnership is quite a different matter (Cornwall 2000).

Thus the term 'partnership' and what it signifies in terms of relationships and practice is open to debate and interpretation. A paper produced for Eurostep (1994), raising questions about implementation and practice, considers partnership to be a pluralist process which may involve stakeholders across a broad spectrum: North–South, North–North, and South–South. It lists aspects of (good) partnership, including the creation of strategic alliances based on common ground, a relationship based on good communication and dialogue between partners who are engaged in a two-way process which is both flexible and transparent. In such a relationship, any disagreements would be negotiated and resolved. According to Cornwall, the challenge for the future is to find a way for those excluded by poverty and discrimination to take up opportunities for influence and control, and to exercise this agency through institutions, spaces, and strategies that they make and shape for themselves.

This chapter investigates the efforts and achievements of an indigenous Southern NGO which has not utilised the term 'partnership', but whose struggle has been and continues to be against the causes of poverty and exclusion and the relations of power that sustain inequalities among indigenous peoples. This perspective from the grassroots, therefore, will explore the nature of alliance building and agenda setting of the indigenous Federation, FENAMAD, in its political struggle for a better-quality and more relevant education for its children.

The Federation recently celebrated its twentieth anniversary by publishing a book containing contributions by some of the many individuals and organisations with whom it has worked over this period. Garcia, writing about the indigenous movement in Madre de Dios, notes how two linked processes brought about the development of the Federation: conflicts between member communities and gold miners invading their lands, and the support that the former received from researchers 'who had sufficient social and political sensitivity and a clear intercultural perspective' to support the communities in their aims for self-development and self-determination (Garcia 2003:278). As other communities experienced similar problems, the need for a collective response was galvanised by the collective traditional view of the world and its influence on their political thinking.

In the 1980s, the Federation persistently lobbied for government recognition of territorial rights for indigenous communities. It addressed serious problems of territorial defence, and human-rights abuses by individuals and by international mining companies. The Federation succeeded in establishing itself as a grassroots indigenous multi-ethnic organisation, linked with AIDESEP (Inter-ethnic Association for the Development of the Peruvian Amazon), an association which at that time comprised four regional federations (and today comprises some 50 organisations). FENAMAD's growth took place at a time when indigenous peoples around the world were organising and becoming a global movement. It forged links with other indigenous organisations in Latin America and the Americas and contributed to the drafting of a Declaration on the Rights of Indigenous Peoples, through the work of the United Nations Working Group on Indigenous Peoples from 1992.

The Federation, therefore, has developed its agenda within a framework of indigenous rights, including rights to education. Education rights are expressed by the indigenous movement in terms of 'indigenous peoples' rights to all levels and forms of education and the right to establish and control their educational systems and institutions providing education in their own language' (draft Declaration on the Rights of Indigenous Peoples, Article 14). At the Earth Summit in 1993, it was declared that

> *indigenous peoples should have the right to their own knowledge, languages and culturally appropriate education including bilingual and bicultural education. Through recognising both formal and informal ways the participation of family and community is guaranteed.*
> (Kari-Oca Declaration, Indigenous Peoples Earth Charter, Brazil 1993)

While the Federation has entered into supportive and co-operative relations with other indigenous organisations at national and international levels, it also works to co-ordinate inter-community and inter-ethnic community relations among its nine different indigenous peoples. The Federation is built upon a direct representational basis, and the elected leadership is answerable to the congress of communities. Gray argues that this kind of organisation, found throughout the Amazon, has scope for working closely with advisers who, with the approval of the congress of community representatives, support and build the capacity of the organisation and its elected leaders (Gray 1996). Thus, the

Federation from its inception has been supported by advisers and concerned anthropologists and others who in a spirit of solidarity have helped it to develop its indigenous rights agenda. But the Federation must also ensure that its relationships and 'partnership' with its base communities are founded on good communications and dialogue.

The Federation has entered into relationships and alliances with a wide range of organisations and actors over two decades, with entry points and agendas defined first and foremost by its demands for rights to self-determination, self-development, territory, culture, language, and identity. Indigenous organisations in Bolivia and Ecuador may be characterised by movements led by their own professionals and intellectuals without the need for mediators (Garcia 2003), but FENAMAD has lacked a formally educated cadre of indigenous professionals. The historical, cultural, geographical, and political situation in Madre de Dios means that the self-development processes of indigenous peoples are associated with other factors, such as their relation with other external agents – anthropologists, national and international NGOs, trade unions, and political parties. In the course of their struggle for recognition of their rights, these relationships have often been paternalistic, assistentialist, and characterised by what Garcia (2003) calls 'a conflictive intercultural dialogue'. Developing and implementing an agenda for indigenous education means, moreover, establishing relations with institutions which have hitherto controlled formal education: the State and the Church. These institutions do not talk in terms of 'partnership' or a 'two-way process of negotiating agendas in a flexible and transparent manner'.

The next sections examine the nature of relations between the Federation and some of these 'external agents', in its efforts to realise rights to education. They trace the development of the Federation's agenda from, initially, demand for access to formal education to a questioning of the quality and relevance of schooling and assertion of the need for indigenous control and decision making in matters of curriculum, language policy, and pedagogy.

Threaded through this examination is the story of Magda. Her experience of education as a girl and young woman is juxtaposed with that of her male contemporaries, and a stark contrast is drawn in terms of the nature of the experience and its relevance to them. Magda is from an indigenous Harakmbut village in the Madre de Dios region of south-east Peru.[2] The Harakmbut peoples are traditionally hunters and gatherers, using the forests and rivers of their lowland rainforest environment for subsistence activities. They are also agriculturists, clearing small areas of the forest to grow manioc, plantains, and a wide variety of tubers and fruits. From the 1970s, three of the communities, of a total of eight, began panning for gold on river banks and in inland alluvial deposits.[3] The Harakmbut peoples today number some 1,500 people; they are one of nine indigenous peoples in the region. Each group has its own way of life, language, values, and bodies of knowledge (Iviche 2003). The exact size of the indigenous population of Madre de Dios is not clear, because there are a number of indigenous people living in 'voluntary isolation', but the total is in the region of 5,000 (Rummenhoeller and Lazarte 1990).

Gender and girls' education in Peru and Madre de Dios

The dominant paradigm of education, focusing on gender equity in access to basic education for all, has produced a distorted view of basic education in many Latin American countries. The EFA Global Monitoring Report confirmed universal primary enrolment for Peru (1999/2000: gross enrolment rates of 128.2 for boys and 126.9 for girls, and a net enrolment rate of 100.00 for both boys and girls). Nevertheless, researchers have for some years now been calling for analysis which goes beyond issues of access to examine the ideological and material structural relations shaping the educational realities in girls' and women's lives (Heward 1999). In the Madre de Dios, in terms of access and retention, girls do as well as boys, perhaps even better in some villages. But this fact obscures a gender-determined dichotomy which, as Magda's story illustrates, has serious consequences in terms of the outcomes of education. Here we are not talking of formal exam results or academic 'success', but of aspects of the cultural and material structural relations to which Heward alludes (ibid.).

The sex-segregated secondary schooling and further education on offer in the Madre de Dios are characterised by two very different ideological and philosophical traditions. While at primary school, in the confines of home and community, both boys and girls experience the influence of Catholic missionary teachers, whose proselytised views were (and to a great extent still are) mediated through informal 'education' within the family and community. However, at secondary level, girls are still subsumed into an hierarchical, authoritarian, and patriarchal mission-based education and way of life through attendance at boarding school. Boys, on the contrary, experience the vagaries of an emerging indigenous political movement, which – despite its (at times) very haphazard attention to the wellbeing of its students – offers a very different education and socialisation from that experienced by girls.

The purpose of this chapter is not to make generalisations about boys' education versus girls' in the region, but rather to follow Magda and her age mates in their different educational trajectories. Magda, because she is a girl, was exposed to the values of a mission organisation for which concepts and practices of partnership and negotiation of agendas are alien concepts. On the contrary, her male contemporaries have experienced changing and fluid practices, as the indigenous organisation responsible for their education negotiates its way towards clarity and recognition of an agenda for achieving indigenous rights through alliances and partnerships with a range of actors. Thus boys are thrust into the political sphere of indigenous politics, while girls are excluded not only from the male political sphere but also from the indigenous political sphere: they are closeted in a female enclave – a convent – within the patriarchal world of the Dominican mission. While Magda may be just as competent to engage with political power as her indigenous brothers – or more so – she is entrusted to a sphere where it is extremely difficult for her to do so. The acceptance of girls' and women's apolitical role confirms what Phillips refers to as the old adage that politics is a man's world (Bourque and Grossholtz 1998:23).

Let us now learn a little about Magda and her experience of education.

Primary schooling

Magda's community first acquired a primary school in the mid-1970s. It was established by the Dominican mission, which employed a local Harakmbut man from the same village who had been educated by Dominican missionaries in the 1960s and groomed to be a leader. Juan taught for several years in the little mission school, which comprised chairs and desks squeezed on to the verandah of his hut. In 1981, he decided to return to his former activities of hunting, fishing, and gold panning and work with his wife in her gardens, in that way achieving some status among his peers (which he did not receive as a teacher). The villagers did not mourn the loss of their indigenous teacher, but took the opportunity to lobby the mission for a Peruvian lay-missionary teacher – believing that this was the hallmark of a 'good' teacher and a 'real' school. In 1983 the community got its teacher, and everyone felt satisfied that their children were getting the Spanish-language education which they had come to believe was 'proper'.

Magda began school in 1983 in the small multi-grade primary school. She was seven years old and joined Grade 1 when the school opened with the new Dominican lay-missionary teacher. It was a one-teacher school with 35 pupils, 22 boys and 13 girls, the vast majority of whom were in Grade 1 – some for the second time, because they had not been considered ready to graduate to Grade 2. The school was now located in a rickety wooden hut with a leaky leaf-thatch roof. The teacher coped alone with all six grades of primary school, teaching each grade in turn. At the end of the year, 13 out of the 16 pupils in Grade 1 failed and were marked down to repeat the year.

Magda herself struggled with Grade 1 for three successive years before qualifying for Grade 2. From 1986, she continued each year up the grades with no more repetitions, until she completed all six grades of primary education. This took her a total of nine years. In the mid-1980s her teacher left, to be replaced by two energetic and dedicated female lay-missionaries who took a pride in improving learning and eradicating grade repetition. They taught in two classes, one teacher with Grades 1 and 2, and the other with Grades 3, 4 ,5 and 6. They lobbied parents to send their children, both boys and girls, to school; and they expected that the girls would produce work of equal quality to that of the boys. By 1990, the village primary school had achieved gender equity in terms of access, retention, and achievement.

Schooling for indigenous girls

The lay-missionary teachers delivered formal education on behalf of the State, which paid their salaries. Community and parents had very little involvement or interest in schooling. These non-indigenous teachers taught the national curriculum in the national language (Spanish) and propagated the national policy of linguistic and cultural assimilation, as well as the Catholic missionaries' brand of religion. For their part, the Harakmbut had to pay the costs of books, pencils, and registration fees for each child and were obliged to maintain the school buildings and teachers' house, and provide fresh food and vegetables for the teachers. Otherwise, most parents had little to do with the processes of schooling and learning within the walls of the school (Aikman 1999a).

The female lay-missionary teachers provided new role models for Harakmbut girls. In sharp contrast to Harakmbut women, the teachers would participate in village meetings and lecture the male community leaders about their 'laziness' and 'backward ways'. They encouraged girls to play basketball, to read, and to speak up for themselves – in short, they encouraged girls to be like them. But in many ways the model of lay-missionary teacher was one of disempowered 'outsider' on the boundary of an indigenous society which they did not understand well and, moreover, were intent on changing and 'developing' according to very different values and practices – including gender relations. The teachers were highly vocal at community meetings, in distinct contrast to Harakmbut women; but in family internal relations, where Harakmbut women have considerable power and influence related to their productive and reproductive roles, the missionary teachers had no voice. The teachers also provided a model of women at the bottom of the Church hierarchy, subject to the control and authority of male missionaries and the all-powerful bishop.

The missionary teachers were further disempowered in an underfunded, centralised, and urban-focused education system which left them dependent on the mercy of traders and itinerant travellers to reach their schools, where they had to stay with little or no contact with teachers in neighbouring communities because of the lack of transport and money. The heavily bureaucratic system, combined with administrative inertia, rendered them unable to take decisions about examination dates; they could not even close the school at end of term until official letters containing the dates of the school terms finally found their way upriver to such remote schools.[4]

Indigenous development and alliances

While Magda laboured at school, the Federation was confronting acutely difficult challenges: land invasions and the indiscriminate plundering of natural resources, violent encounters with colonists, and exploitative relations with authorities. Its attempts to tackle these threats were accompanied by a growing awareness of a lack of educational qualifications, not only among the all-male leadership of the Federation but also among young people in general. As demands on the Federation grew, so too did the need for indigenous capacity in a wide range of areas, not least in competent literacy skills in Spanish. The Federation lobbied for the provision of primary schools in all communities. Harakmbut communities were predominantly served by the missionary network, but others came under the direct control of the Ministry of Education. The schools of the latter, where they existed, suffered greatly from teacher absenteeism and high turnover.

At its first Congress in 1982, it was noted that 70 young people had completed primary schooling; but there were no secondary schools in any of the indigenous communities, so to pursue further study young people had to leave home for the regional town or attend a Dominican mission school outside the region. The Federation leadership was aware of the challenge of asserting their rights in a society prejudiced against them. Leaders with only a few years of primary education were not taken seriously and had to struggle to gain any respect from local authorities, who equated indigenous identity with ignorance.

Building the capacity of the Federation and indigenous youth became a priority for the Federation through the 1980s. Some grants were secured from the regional authority for secondary schooling and, at the beginning of the 1990s, four youths who had completed secondary education began to study in Lima for the university entrance exams, aided by grants from the Norwegian Development Ministry (NORAD). Meanwhile, the Federation felt disempowered by a lack of indigenous capacity in a range of areas – accounting, administration, agro-forestry, and land-demarcation processes as well as law, medicine, and, of course, education. It relied on non-indigenous technical expertise – some of which was provided by supporters and solidarity organisations. Through the 1980s the Federation grew in strength, supported by the Eori Centre, an NGO which comprised non-indigenous professionals and put its services at the disposal of the Federation and planned its work around the priority themes arising from its congresses: recognition and titling of indigenous communities, defence and consolidation of communal territories, defence of human and civil rights, education, health services, and organisational issues (Garcia 2003).

Over this period the Federation was also developing relations with other indigenous organisations in Peru and strengthening links with South American indigenous organisations and with organisations from North American and English-speaking parts of the globe (see Gray 1997). It formed a strong alliance on common causes with the non-indigenous Agrarian Federation of Madre de Dios (FADEMAD) and took part in, for example, a strike against a unilateral revaluation of agriculturists' debts to the Agrarian Bank, agreements in support of the titling of indigenous lands, and the newly established Coordination for the Conservation of Madre de Dios to fight for the establishment of indigenous reserves to protect traditional territory from depredation through timber and oil extraction (Garcia 2003). These strategic alliances have allowed the organisation to increase its impact and gain political respect from government institutions in Madre de Dios, although the nature of the political space has varied under different national political regimes.

By its seventh congress in 1991, the Federation was mandated to deal with a range of educational demands, which included lobbying for primary schools in some of its communities (FENAMAD 1991). At the time, there was a growing awareness of the problematic nature of formal education provided by missions and the State, in that it was linguistically and culturally inappropriate for indigenous children. A study carried out in the region noted that 90 per cent of teachers working in indigenous communities had little or no training, and some lacked complete secondary education (Rummenhoeller and Lazarte 1991). While the study noted that lay-missionary teachers were more dedicated to their work than teachers hired by the Ministry of Education, their criteria for good teaching were not always compatible with those of the indigenous communities (ibid:169).

Secondary schooling

The Federation at its seventh congress was also mandated to pursue a demand for the creation of an indigenous secondary school in a community of the Shipibo people, and to secure more grants to allow students to attend secondary school in Puerto Maldonado. Statistics for 1983–1990 reveal a marked bias towards grants for boys (32 boys and 6 girls receiving them over this period).

Rummenhoeller and Lazarte (1991) explain that parents were afraid that away from home their daughters might run off with non-indigenous men; that more boys completed primary schooling; and that the policy of the Federation and local authority favoured boys.

The First Meeting of Indigenous Women in Madre de Dios took place in 1990 to address the issue of the 'alienation of indigenous women through the processes of contact with western society and the introduction of new ideas and values which have led to changes in the way we are and think' (FENAMAD 1990). The meeting's concern with education was expressed in terms of the quality of schooling for children in general.

Magda's generation of primary-school graduates benefited from the Federation's lobbying of the regional authorities for increased access to secondary schooling and from increased demand at the community level. There was increasing awareness that a formal primary education did not provide indigenous girls or boys with new skills and knowledge which they could use in their communities, at a time when the traditional economic pursuits of hunting and fishing were becoming unsustainable because of destruction of the environment by the gold-panning activities of increasing numbers of colonists. Parents expected formal education to provide skills and qualifications for alternative economic activities, although it was quickly clear that primary schooling alone could not provide this – and thus parents' expectations of secondary schooling were raised. Teachers urged parents to send their children to secondary school; to ensure that female students could also take advantage of this opportunity, the lay-missionary teachers working in Harakmbut schools lobbied the Diocese for boarding facilities for girls and lobbied the local authority for grants. The regional authority provided grants, which the Federation administered for boys and the Diocese for girls.

Magda's convent boarding school

In 1991 Magda left home for secondary school: she was to board in a Dominican convent and live behind high walls and locked doors with the nuns, attending mass twice a day, while her male contemporaries boarded in the rough accommodation of the Federation's new head office. The boys entered a world of indigenous politics, ethnic tensions, political debate, and engagement with the indigenous movement. Delays in the arrival of funds to the Federation meant that the boys sometimes went hungry, and there was often no money for books, no light at night for studying, and no water for washing. But they had the freedom to experience the excitement as well as the dangers and racism of non-indigenous society in the small frontier town. (Indigenous students attended single-sex State schools.)

Magda's family effectively handed over complete responsibility for her welfare to the Dominican nuns, whose educational agenda for young indigenous girls continued in the vein of the lay-missionary primary school, to the extent that they promoted excellence in educational achievement, a dedication to Christ and the Church, and servility and domestication in their role as young women. The girls' physical welfare was secure, but their spiritual and cultural development diverged from that of their male counterparts, who were plunged into a world of indigenous political struggle, in direct contact with people from all the ethnic groups in the region, as well as close contact with solidarity organisations such as the Eori Centre, and individuals committed to the indigenous movement, such as anthropologists and sociologists, which exposed them to debate, discussion, and active engagement.

For both boys and girls, however, the rate of drop-out from secondary school was high. The contrast with life in the indigenous communities was stark, and home lay several days' journey away by canoe, a costly and exhausting journey. Magda's classmate from her village ran away before the end of the first year, unable to endure the ascetic conditions of the convent. Another friend then ran away to find work as a cook in a settlers' gold camp in squalid conditions by the river bank. Contrary to parents' optimistic but uninformed hopes for brighter futures, the curriculum and religious teachings of the school did nothing to encourage these young women to return to their communities on completion. With deteriorating economic conditions in the communities, home held a limited attraction for girls who had already assimilated many of the customs and values of the capitalist money-oriented town life. For her part, Magda chose to stay in the convent during holiday periods, rather than take the long canoe trip up-river to her home and family, where she felt increasingly out of place.

Beginning to question formal education

In other parts of the rainforest, indigenous organisations had been formulating demands for a different kind of formal education for indigenous children. A study carried out for the Inter-ethnic Association for the Development of the Amazon (AIDESEP), an Amazon-wide indigenous umbrella organisation in eight regions of the Amazon, provided evidence of the poor quality of education and high rates of drop-out and alienation among school children. Chirif (1991:66) notes that 'formal schooling destroys the processes of learning and socialisation taking place within communities and families. Schooling is nothing short of ethnocidal.' As access to formal education at primary and secondary levels slowly increased during the 1980s, there was a growing crisis of confidence among indigenous organisations in the ability of formal State schooling to provide the knowledge, skills, and attitudes that indigenous students needed to confront their rapidly changing social and physical environment and shape it according to their indigenous values and beliefs. On the contrary, formal schooling was contributing to the loss of social and cultural values; hopes of having indigenous teachers, as well as lawyers, doctors, nurses, and accountants, were 'an illusion' when the majority of indigenous children left primary school barely able to read and write (Trapnell 2003) and had no opportunities for secondary education at all.

Training teachers for indigenous education

Developments in intercultural and bilingual education

While FENAMAD was still a fledgling organisation in the southern Amazon region, the member organisations of AIDESEP in the northern Amazon had been drawing on their own cadres of indigenous teachers and developing alliances which resulted in a dynamic partnership between AIDESEP and a team of non-indigenous linguists, anthropologists, and educators. A fruitful collaboration with the Loreto Teacher Training College and the University of Iquitos Centre for Anthropological Research produced a radically new intercultural teacher-training course for bilingual indigenous teachers working at the primary-school level. It was founded on the needs and demands of the indigenous peoples themselves, and developed through a partnership based on strong common goals, linked to the recognition, defence, and promotion of indigenous rights (Trapnell 2003). The programme (referred to as the AIDESEP / ISPL programme) achieved institutional recognition from the teacher-training college where it was located (Loreto), and brought with it much of its own external funding from an international NGO (Terra Nova). This brought a degree of autonomy necessary for the design and implementation not only of the teacher-training course but of a bilingual and intercultural primary-education curriculum for indigenous children which was later given government recognition.

As the Federation in the southern rainforest slowly made gains in terms of access to formal schooling, it began to turn its attention also to critiques of State and mission education. Researchers worked with members of the Federation to draft proposals for teacher training and curriculum development for bilingual education. Visits were made to the project in Loreto, to talk with the team and learn from this new model of education. However, the Federation faced stiff resistance to any suggestion of an alternative teacher-training or primary curriculum from the Dominican mission, which still controlled basic services in the Madre de Dios region. The political space for the Federation to develop and express its ideas for an alternative to formal State/mission schooling was severely constrained by Church and State. The Diocese was in a powerful alliance with the regional education authorities, who believed that the best education for indigenous children was one that assimilated them into the economic life of the nation as quickly as possible (Aikman 1999c).

Magda at teacher-training college

In 1996 Magda completed secondary school, and the missionaries offered her the chance to study at the Puerto Maldonado Teacher Training College to become a primary teacher. As a trainee teacher, she now moved from the direct tutelage of the nuns in the convent to board with the lay-missionaries in their hostel.

Magda graduated as the first trained teacher in her village – but she had been trained to teach a monocultural assimilationist curriculum which perceived indigenous children as in need of being 'developed' and integrated into the wider society. She was faced with difficult choices for her future. She had spent nearly two decades tied to an education system that was inimical to her people's way of life and values. Her indigenous friends and contemporaries who had begun formal schooling with her were now married and had children. Her years away at school and college and her high levels of formal education meant that it would be difficult for her to find a husband in her village: the eligible men – already a small pool because of strict kinship rules – had matured in a very different environment from her. The Ministry of Education posted its teachers on an annual basis, and it was not clear that Magda would be appointed to work in her own village or even a village belonging to her ethnic and linguistic group, the Harakmbut.

Mainstream teacher training versus indigenous teacher training

While it is not possible here to assess in detail the quality of the training that Magda received in the mid-late 1990s, a study of the overall quality and orientation of initial training at that time in State teacher-training institutes raises questions (Palacios 1997). The 1990s was a time of piecemeal reform of education, with teacher training lagging behind reform of the primary system and the introduction of a competency-based curriculum from 1996. Teachers received short, one-off in-service training courses, while the introduction of a new ethos and approach to initial teacher training was developed later. Intercultural education was introduced as a 'cross-cutting theme' in the primary curriculum, and some Andean colleges offered the ministry's Curriculum Model for Regular and In-service training in Bilingual Intercultural Education (MOFEBI); but this course was authorised by the ministry with no specific training for the college and teachers involved, and the majority of teachers simply did not know what intercultural bilingual education meant (Trapnell 2003). It was not implemented in the institution at Puerto Maldonado, where Magda studied.

In 1998 the Bilingual Teacher Training Programme developed in Loreto by AIDESEP/ISPL received funding from the European Union to expand its model beyond the northern Peruvian Amazon through a project called 'FORTE –PE'. FENAMAD, still unable to further its aims for developing its own intercultural bilingual teacher training and primary education, was keen to engage via this programme. However, negotiations with the Ministry of Education advanced slowly, as bureaucratic discussions about resources and procedures over-whelmed discussion of what interculturalism means in a multi-ethnic region with a plurality of indigenous peoples. The challenge of introducing a competency-based approach and child-focused pedagogy took precedence over questions of knowledge, meaning, and indigenous identity. Unlike the relationship in the north, in Madre de Dios the Ministry of Education and the local college staff (either lay-missionaries themselves, or taught and trained by them) were unwilling or unable to enter into a new type of relationship: co-leadership by the Federation, its education team, and the college and ministry staff. The programme was stifled by the college bureaucracy, and there seemed little hope for a new training centre, intended to be primarily under indigenous control.

While Magda was slowly but steadily progressing through the formal State education system under the sex-segregated control of the missionaries, the indigenous Federation's politics of education had come to focus more clearly on intercultural bilingual education and the need to train indigenous youth to be bilingual intercultural teachers. However, for the Dominican Diocese and the Ministry of Education, the introduction of intercultural education meant making superficial changes to the national curriculum, in a context where the political will for developing a common agenda and goals was ambiguous. The success of indigenous-defined intercultural education demands a partnership built on transparency, flexibility, negotiation, and mutual learning.[5] As Trapnell notes, the barriers confronting intercultural bilingual education are a dramatic expression of the predominance of social and political models based on the exclusion of certain peoples and social groups, and the lack of democratic principles and practice (Trapnell 2003:181).

For the success of intercultural bilingual education in Madre de Dios, the Federation depended for support on those who were committed to the principles of the indigenous movement, who solidly identified with their background and values, and who would take up the fight for a new kind of indigenous education. Magda's education and training had led her along a very different path, which meant that her considerable achievement in this formal system had distanced her from indigenous politics. Her long formal education had preached the superiority of non-indigenous knowledge and the superiority of the written word over oral wisdom; she had been led to believe that indigenous ways of life and beliefs are antithetical to 'modern life', and that 'indigenous' is backward-looking and 'Peruvian' is forward-looking. To work with an indigenous-controlled intercultural education, she would have to fight against much of what she had been taught in school, while embedded in the world of the missionaries. As an indigenous woman who speaks her local language and has strong emotional ties to her family, she has a lot to offer. As a formally trained teacher, she is one of the few who has Ministry of Education certification to teach in a State school. Her particular training has inculcated skills and knowledge which are valuable for her people – as well as values and knowledge which run contrary to her people's spirituality and their political agenda for self-determination. But with support and motivation, Magda could overcome this polarised view of the world, and her sense of the value of her indigenousness could be nurtured through training as an intercultural bilingual teacher. Today indigenous peoples move between diverse social and cultural contexts, and they need an education which equips them for this challenging and fast- changing environment.

Conclusion

The AIDESEP / ISPL programme was designed in the mid-1980s at a moment when indigenous peoples began to challenge State education as 'ethnocidal', a time when the concept of intercultural education was being developed in the Amazon and Andean regions. Now the government and Ministry of Education have mainstreamed 'interculturalism', and in the process the issue has lost it radical edge. The concepts associated with it, such as dialogue, negotiation, and respect for diversity are 'encountering severe limitations at the practical and operative level' (Trapnell 2003:181). Thus the expansion of the AIDESEP / ISPL model to the Federation and the indigenous peoples of Madre de Dios via Church and State institutions has debilitated the practices of dialogue and negotiation, based on respect for indigenous peoples, on which this model rests. It has encountered the inability of Church and State institutions to work in a partnership founded on 'common ground and a relationship based on good communication and dialogue between partners engaged in a two-way process which is both flexible and transparent' (Eurostep 1994). It has been constricted by nationally prescribed competencies and pedagogical practices which exclude indigenous values and knowledge. And finally it has encountered a lack of commitment to interculturalism as a process of dialogue and negotiation towards the development of more just relations.

Magda's story illustrates the fact that girls' education and gender equality were not at the forefront of demands and developments for the Federation through the 1980s and 1990s. The foreword to a volume entitled *Indigenous Women: The Right to a Voice* pertinently notes:

> While indigenous women affirm their specific, practical gender needs, their overall strategic interests – at this point of time – very much coincide with those of their men: the right to land and self-determination and the respect of human rights. And what they claim is to be at the side of their men in the struggle for these rights.
>
> (Vinding 1998:14).

Indigenous women of Madre de Dios recognised their alienated positions and the need to reclaim indigenous learning and knowledge within the household and the community (FENAMAD 1990), but they have not been empowered to work with the male-dominated Federation to demand equality and recognition of women's indigenous knowledge and learning in the formal education system. While the Federation has campaigned for more access to education, and more recently for intercultural education, there has been little or no questioning of the impact of the gendered nature of formal schooling – both in content and structure – on their girls and boys, nor of the double discrimination experienced by young women like Magda in a system controlled by the Church.

In a continent where gender equity is said to have been achieved in terms of educational access and achievement, it is not easy to raise concerns about the nature of the formal educational experience for girls. Concerns for the physical safety of girls studying away from home have over-ridden a questioning of the messages and values being inculcated through participation in a national assimilationist education system and through missionary proselytisation. What Magda gained in terms of physical security she lost in terms of security of her identity and place in her indigenous society: her motivation as part of the collective thrust towards the achievement of rights to land and a sustainable future based on collective indigenous values. Instead she was encouraged to develop her individual sense of responsibility to Church, State, and school. The extent to which she can reconcile or accommodate these two views of the world remains to be seen.

This chapter has considered the nature of partnerships and alliances into which the indigenous Federation has entered over its twenty-year struggle for indigenous rights. It has focused on the campaign for rights to intercultural education, in a context where indigenous people directly experience prejudice and exclusion. It has emphasised the need for the organisation to ensure that its agenda, policies, and practice incorporate a thorough gender analysis. It has also provided an illustration of the types of alliance and partnership and relations that the Federation has forged in the course of its struggle to assert the rights of indigenous people in the south-eastern Amazon region of Peru. While the

Federation has achieved some laudable successes, this chapter has also drawn attention to the extent and pervasiveness of inequalities in education and difficulties inherent in forging partnerships with State and Church institutions to change this situation. The struggle for an intercultural education which meets the needs and threats faced by indigenous men and women in Madre de Dios will not, however, be achieved until State and Church recognise the need to respect indigenous peoples and work alongside them as equals.

Sheila Aikman, Education Policy Adviser with Oxfam GB, was previously a lecturer in Education and International Development at the Institute of Education, University of London. She has carried out ethnographic fieldwork in the Peruvian Amazon with the Harakmbut peoples and has published extensively on intercultural bilingual education and indigenous education in Latin America.

Notes

1   FENAMAD: Federación Nativa del Río Madre de Dios y Afluentes. The Department of Madre de Dios is located in the south-east of Peru and is a region of lowland tropical rainforest with some areas of Andes foothills.

2   'Magda' is a pseudonym.

3   Details of the Harakmbut peoples and their way of life can be found in Gray 1996; Moore 2003; Aikman 1999a.

4   For more details of schooling for girls under the control of missionaries in this region, see Aikman 1999b.

5   For a discussion of the challenges of the political negotiations in which the AIDESEP / ISPL programme now finds itself, see Trapnell 2003.

References

Aikman, S. (1999a) *Language, Literacy and Bilingual Education*, Amsterdam: Benjamins.

Aikman, S. (1999b) 'Schooling and development: eroding Amazon women's knowledge and diversity' in C. Heward and S. Bunwaree (eds.) *Gender, Education and Development: Beyond Access to Empowerment*, London: Zed, 1999.

Aikman, S. (1999c) 'Alternative development and education: economic interests and cultural practices in the Amazon', in A. Little and F. Leach (eds.) *Education, Culture and Economics: Dilemmas for Development*, New York: Falmer Press.

Bourque, S. and J. Grossholtz (1998) 'Politics an unnatural practice: political science looks at female participation', in A. Phillips (ed.) *Feminism and Politics*, Oxford: Oxford University Press.

Chirif, A. (1991) 'Contexto y Caracteristicas de la Educación Oficial en Sociedades Indígenas (Amazonía peruana)' in M. Zúñiga, I. Pozzi-Escot and L.E. López (eds.) *Educación Bilingue Intercultural: reflexiones y desafíos*, Lima: Fomciencias.

Cornwall, A. (2000) *Beneficiary, Consumer, Citizen: Perspectives on Participation for Poverty Reduction*, SIDA Studies, 2.

Eurostep (1994) *Gender in Partnership*, Eurostep Gender Workshop 2, MSC.

FENAMAD (1990) 'Informe del Primer Encuentro de Mujeres Nativas de Madre de Dios', unpublished report.

FENAMAD (1991) 'Conclusiones del VII Congreso', unpublished report.

Garcia, A. Altamirano (2003) 'FENAMAD 20 Años después: Apuntes sobre el movimiento indígena amazónico en Madre de Dio' in B. Huertas Castillo and A. Garcia Altamirano (eds.) *Los Pueblos Indígenas de Madre de Dios: historia, etnografía y coyuntura*, Copenhagen: IWGIA.

Gray, A. (1996) *Y después de la fiebre del oro…? Derechos Humanos y Autodeterminación entre los Amarakaeri del Sudeste del Perú*, Copenhagen: IWGIA.

Gray, A. (1997*) Indigenous Rights and Development: Self-determination in an Amazon Community*, Oxford: Berghahn.

Hauck, V. and T. Land (2000) *Beyond Partnership Rhetoric: Reviewing Experiences and Policy Considerations for Implementing Genuine Partnerships in North–South Co-operation*, Discussion Paper No. 20, European Centre for Development Policy Management.

Heward, C. (1999) Introduction to *Gender, Education, and Development: Beyond Access to Empowerment* (C. Heward and S. Bunwaree, eds.), London, Zed Books, 1999.

Iviche, A. Quique (2003) 'Prólogo', in B. Huertas Castillo and A. Garcia Altamirano (eds.) *Los Pueblos Indígenas de Madre de Dios: historia, etnografía y coyuntura*, Copenhagen: IWGIA.

Moore, T. (2003) 'La etnografía tradicional Arakmbut y la minería aurifea' in B. Huertas Castillo and A. Garcia Altamirano (eds.) *Los Pueblos Indígenas de Madre de Dios: historia, etnografía y coyuntura*, Copenhagen: IWGIA.

Palacios, M. A. (1997) *Consideraciones para una Política de Desarrollo Magisterial*, Lima: Foro Educativo.

Rummenhoeller, K. and M. Lazarte Velarde (1990) 'Comunidades Indígenas de Madre de Dios (Perú): un enfoque de la realidad educativa', *América Indígena* 4:159-92.

Sueyo, H. Yumbuyo (2003) 'Educational Biography of an Arakmbut', *Comparative Education* 39(2): 193-8.

Trapnell, L. (2003) 'Some key issues in intercultural bilingual education teacher training programmes – as seen from a teacher training programme in the Peruvian Amazon Basin', *Comparative Education* Special Issue on Indigenous Education, 39 (2):165-84.

Vinding, D. (1998) 'Foreword' in D. Vinding (ed.) *Indigenous Women: the Right to a Voice*, Copenhagen: IWGIA.

Part Three

Scaling Up and Sustainability

7 Innovation and mediation: the case of Egypt

Malak Zaalouk

In recent decades, development policy makers have made a stronger commitment to the concept of partnerships and various forms of participation. This commitment stems from certain theoretical and philosophical positions, as well as practical political stances.

In terms of education theory, it has become evident that individual learners have complex needs, and that, in order to achieve high-quality learning, those needs, and the complex nature of the context in which learning takes place, must be addressed. Consequently, there is a growing recognition of the need for multi-sector approaches to education. On a more philosophical level, post-modernist thinking suggests that, in an increasingly uncertain world, planning and management must be adaptive. There is a need for leadership styles and methods which can forge partnerships, delegate power and authority for greater flexibility, and mobilise and catalyse a wide array of partners to reach desired objectives. On the political level, most governments in developing countries have accepted that the model of a strong welfare state is gradually withering away. Nevertheless, states with weakened structures and limited means have pledged themselves to attain global development goals. They have therefore welcomed the idea of engaging in wide-ranging partnerships to achieve their national goals and objectives.

While the invitation to engage in partnerships may be viewed as a pragmatic solution to persistent social and economic developmental constraints and failures, it has nonetheless allowed a certain degree of empowerment both to civil society and to communities at large. It is helping to foster the genesis of a new era of potential democracy and public accountability, one in which partnerships can be authentic. Engaging in public affairs is no longer limited to narrowly specified domains; nor can it, in the long run, be treated as an optional activity. This is creating a dynamic which might indeed change the configuration of existing power relations, on both the national and the international scenes.

A global movement for girls' education

A global movement for girls' education is manifesting itself through increased attention to gender issues, which could lead to significant social and political changes. It is a movement which aims to transform power relationships – not only between male and female, but also between learner and teacher, and between communities and official government structures. It is a movement which brings to the fore a new paradigm for learning and a new positioning of communities in the management of their lives and their children's learning. It is, moreover, a movement which fosters growing partnerships.

This chapter will trace the development of the modern movement for girls' education in Egypt within the context of the global movement for girls' education in the 1990s. It will focus on the role of community schools in initiating a movement for good-quality education for girls in Egypt. It will describe the processes through which – almost a decade later – the United Nations Girls' Education Initiative (UNGEI) found fertile ground in Egypt and resulted in the Egypt Girls' Education Movement (EGEI). Inspired by the community-school model at the national level and UNGEI at the international level, the Egypt Girls' Education Initiative seeks to develop partnerships through which government and communities can work together.

This chapter will explore in particular how such partnerships between local communities, non-government organisations (NGOs), and government have been fostered to promote girls' education through the mediation of UNICEF. UNICEF's role in the community schools initiative is seen as that of a catalyst and mediator between government and communities, a role that it continues to play in the Egypt Girls' Education Initiative. This chapter will examine the nature of the partnerships formed in each instance, with a focus on the roles of each partner. It will also attempt to offer an analytical assessment of such partnerships, and the mediation role played by UNICEF within the context of current efforts to scale up the achievements of the girls' education movement.

The context of girls' education in Egypt

Concern for girls' education has had a long history in Egypt, beginning more than a century ago with the establishment of separate schools for girls. Civil society was a partner in the reform of education during the nationalist struggle against colonialism: the first university – Cairo University – was in fact founded by community members, with opportunities open to women. Schools grew up rapidly during the 1950s and 1960s under a policy of compulsory and free basic education for all, with gender equity in enrolments guaranteed in the

Constitution. But economic setbacks in the 1970s and 1980s resulted in limited investments in education, deteriorating infrastructure, and significant gaps between opportunities provided to boys and opportunities offered to girls.

Significant progress in girls' education was registered in the 1990s: concerted efforts resulted in a reduction in the gender gap in gross primary enrolment rates from 12 percentage points in 1990 to 3 percentage points by 2001/2002. A gender gap of just 3 percentage points also characterises gross enrolment rates at preparatory and secondary levels. Such national averages, however, mask significant regional disparities, particularly in the governorates of Upper Egypt in the south, where overall enrolments remain lower, and gender gaps in primary net enrolments range up to 15.7 percentage points. Table 1 shows the gender gaps in some governorates with the widest gaps.

Table 1: Primary education in Egypt – the gender gap per governorate

Governorate	Gender gap
Bani Soueif	15.7%
Assiut	14.2%
El-Minya	13.4%
Fayoum	12.6%
Sohag	11%
El Beheira	3.2%
El Guiza	2.5%

Analyses conducted in the seven governorates featured in Table 1 indicated clearly that poverty was the main reason for families' failure to send their daughters to school. Most families were not able to pay the direct costs of schooling. If they did send their girls to school, the opportunity costs were great: girls performed valuable household chores and were often able to earn more income for the family than boys were. This was particularly true in the fishing industry, where the 'nimble fingers' of girls were much in demand for cleaning and peeling sardines and shrimp. High overall unemployment and limited prospects for either school or college graduates further discouraged parental investment in education, as did the very scarcity and poor quality of schools in remote communities. Concerns about safety and security were an issue in some areas, and practices of early marriage constituted an additional factor that restricted education for girls, which was seen as a potential threat to male and parental authority.

Taken together, these factors added up to limited educational opportunities for girls – a problem that the community schools were set up to address.

The community school initiative

The community schools programme was established in 1992 through a partnership between the Ministry of Education, UNICEF, and local communities. The programme aimed to reach girls in deprived rural areas where the gender gap was high: in governorates of Upper Egypt such as Assiut, Sohag, and Qena. It targeted children in hard-to-reach hamlets who had never been to school. It was designed to provide formal primary education through high-quality learning in child-friendly (and especially girl-friendly) schools, relying heavily on community participation and innovative methods in so doing. This marked the genesis of the girls' education initiative in Egypt.

The first four schools were established in Assiut governorate in the district of Manfalout in the villages of Bani Shokeir, Om al Kossour, and Bani Rafei. After a few years, schools were established in various districts in the governorates of Sohag and Qena, and a new district in Assiut called Abou Teeg. From the beginning, the communities were considered the main partners in the initiative. They were to be responsible for providing safe and child-friendly learning spaces for girls within the community, and would also be responsible for sustaining, maintaining, and running those schools. Communities in addition nominated facilitators/teachers, mostly young women from the villages who had completed an intermediate-level education. The Ministry of Education would participate in the selection of facilitators and pay their salaries. The ministry would ensure that schoolbooks and school meals were supplied to those hard-to-reach areas, and it would act in partnership with NGOs to supervise the schools. UNICEF was responsible for designing the initiative, conducting training, providing furniture, equipment, and stationery, and (with other partners) supervising, monitoring, and evaluating the schools.

Diffusion of the community education model

From the four initial schools established during the pilot stage, community schools blossomed during the course of the decade, numbering 202 by 2000 and reaching 8,000 children – 70 per cent of them girls. Moreover, community schools provided a diffusive model which was taken up and applied by others, such that by the end of the 1990s there were more than 3,500 similar schools, reaching close to 80,000 children, 80 per cent of them girls.

In 1993, in the first step towards scaling up the community-school initiative, the Ministry of Education established an associated programme, known as the

One-Room School Initiative, which targeted girls who had dropped out of school. It focused on vocational training, in addition to offering formal primary education. From an initial total of 213 one-room schools in 1993/1994, the programme expanded to 2,649 such schools in 2001/2002.

In 1994, with training from UNICEF, the Social Fund for Development (SFD) established another 150 community schools through partnerships with NGOs. The SFD community schools continue to expand to date. Several NGOs established the model in a number of governorates. Meanwhile, in 1997, USAID, in partnership with the Ministry of Education, set up the New School programme in three governorates of Upper Egypt, basing it on the model of community schools. By 2002, such new schools numbered 45. At almost the same time, the World Bank and the European Union, through a Planning Programme Monitoring Unit (PPMU), engaged in a similar initiative for what they called 'Second Chance' education through community mobilisation.

Each phase of the programme – pilot, development, and expansion – attracted more and more partners. NGOs, local universities, and specialised institutions joined the partnership, with a particular concern to support training programmes and curriculum development. Moreover, other donor agencies offered support; the Canadian International Development Agency (CIDA), for example, became a strong partner. Private individuals and the private sector proper also joined the partnership and provided financial support.

'Community Education' was the name given by the Ministry of Education to all the initiatives that adopted the community school model, indicating that such initiatives were not discrete programmes or pilot projects, but part of a movement initiated by the community schools and fully adopted and led by the Ministry of Education. Community schools had been recognised as a leading model for community ownership and quality learning.

Partnerships within the community school model

Through its support for the initial community school model, UNICEF had catalysed and mediated a partnership between local communities, NGOs, and government. The experience was largely successful, because both government and communities trusted UNICEF. After some initial reluctance, the government eventually saw great value in communities' active support for national educational goals of universal primary education. Communities, on the other hand, were eager to be recognised and to acquire formal education for their children. UNICEF worked hard both to negotiate the partnership and to enhance all parties' capacity for participation.

In response to this new and much-needed trend, the Ministry of Education established a directorate to manage and co-ordinate on-going partnerships with NGOs wishing to support schools. The government also showed an interest in mainstreaming the participatory elements in the model, such as the education committees (described below) and the selection and recruitment of female facilitators from the local community.

Community education committees

The most significant partner in the community school model is the education committee, which is broadly representative of the communities in each of the sites. In earlier initiatives, communities had typically been invited to donate land and money for schools and other services. This time, however, while communities were still invited to make contributions in cash and kind, they were also encouraged to plan for and manage the schools.

In Assiut, Sohag, and Qena, the three governorates of Upper Egypt where the initiative took root, education committees were carefully groomed by UNICEF staff, in partnership with NGOs. A lengthy process of dialogue helped to create a spirit of trust and rapport over the months and years. With UNICEF working as mediator through NGOs, the committees were able to network and connect with responsible government officials at the village and district levels. The ensuing partnerships have been largely harmonious and collaborative.

Education committees make major decisions concerning the selection of sites for schools, the selection of teachers/facilitators, and the shape of the school schedule. They have enriched the curricula and solved problems related to the school and local communities. More importantly, they organise and govern themselves and the communities in which the schools were established. As a result of their work with community schools, education committees have attained a better position to claim other services for their hamlets, such as roads, electricity, and safe drinking water.

The men, women, and young people who comprise the education committees are largely agricultural workers and small farmers from very poor and deprived backgrounds. Some are the parents of the would-be pupils. Others are simply active and concerned members of the community. They are mostly illiterate, especially the women, and have never participated in public life before. Through the initiative they have been intensively trained, sensitised, and consequently empowered.

Women are important members of the education committees, making up 30 per cent of the membership. They have been selected and engaged through assertive action by the UNICEF teams. At times, when necessary, they meet separately from men, but in most situations they participate with the men in making critical decisions about their communities. Participation in the education committees has enabled them to become active and mobile. At last, after being silent and invisible for so long, their voices are being heard, and they have been able to move into the public domain.

Overall, this remarkably effective partnership with communities has shown policy makers what people can do: they can indeed participate in setting up schools of the highest standard in hard-to-reach areas where government is not easily able to penetrate. They are saving government funds, but they are slowly growing more and more autonomous and are very gradually moving from a marginal position to one of empowerment. During an evaluation of the initiative, the communities were clearly quite conscious of the role that they were playing, and confident that if need be they would find ways of sustaining their schools without external assistance.[1]

Teachers/facilitators and supervisors

Other important partners in the initiative are the facilitators/teachers, who are drawn from the local communities, and the teams of supervisors who represent NGOs. The facilitators are essentially young women – largely unemployed – who have completed intermediate education and are intensively trained through the initiative to become primary-school teachers, with salaries paid by the Ministry of Education. The supervisors, also young women from the three governorates of Assiut, Sohag, and Qena, have obtained higher education and are leaders in the initiative. Both facilitators and supervisors have been instrumental in developing the initiative. They have furthermore been able to negotiate certain benefits for themselves and the children from a position of power. Recently, for example, the facilitators have explored the possibility of establishing a professional association to safeguard their rights.

The relationship between the Ministry of Education and the facilitators has been far more complex than that between the ministry and local communities, and it has been characterised by several phases of acceptance and rejection. Although the para-professionals are paid by the ministry in accordance with the agreement negotiated in 1992, officials at the ministry initially found it hard to accept them as the equivalents of graduates from faculties of education and teachers' colleges. Gradually, however, the effectiveness and professionalism of these young women have been demonstrated by the results of several evaluations of the community schools, and also by the level of children's achievement. Facilitators have thus become respected as model teachers by ministry officials.

The most recent evaluation, conducted in 2001, indicated that facilitators of the community schools had acquired the knowledge, skills, and attitudes needed for the effective management of classes with high-performing students.[2] Now it is not uncommon for MoE directorates at the governorate levels to seek to employ facilitators of the community schools in official government schools. Currently, the MoE has established a policy of equivalence, to allow the provincial directorates to appoint the community schools facilitators after three years of experience and training.

Contribution to educational reform

The facilitators and supervisors have become strong partners in Egypt's education-reform programme, launched as a follow-up to the Dakar World Education Forum as a means of improving the quality of education. The reform focuses on child-centred, activity-based learning, with the country developing its own standards for the outcomes of learning, teacher performance, school and classroom management, and community participation.

Over the past five years, community school facilitators and supervisors/ support mentors have become partners in the development of activity-based curricula, as members of technical teams from the community schools who have been invited to advise the Center for Curriculum and Instructional Materials Development (CCIMD). They are showing the way forward in the creation of attractive materials for multi-ability and multi-grade teaching which take into account diverse styles of learning and stimulate students of differing intellectual abilities. Through their guidance, new materials are being developed. They are able to work with ease as a result of the partnerships fostered with the learners in their own classrooms.

Children are a great source of inspiration to the facilitators. They are partners in the management and discipline of their classrooms. Children and their facilitators agree on some objectives of learning and then they create materials to support the objectives. Rules of behaviour in the school and classroom discipline are governed by a 'social contract' or 'learning contract', and a partnership is sealed which recognises the rights of the children.

The community school teams (facilitators and supervisors) are also partners in training, as they spread their philosophy in the training sessions that they jointly attend with other government teachers and supervisors. They take it upon themselves to spread the philosophy of their schools to other regular schools in nearby districts. They are indeed partners in diffusing their participatory model to other educational institutions.

It is thus through an intricate web of partnerships that community schools carefully ensure the sustainability of the movement. The wider the partnerships, the greater the opportunity for sustainable growth. The partnerships in the movement, and the very strong networks that have been established, have created an unparalleled sense of ownership by communities and a wide demand for high-quality teaching. Recognising this, government and high-level policy makers have adopted the community school model as a source of new ideas, deserving wider diffusion. The model has moreover been selected as the way forward for increasing girls' access to education, achieving greater equity, and ensuring higher quality through the Egypt Girls' Education Initiative.

The Egypt Girls' Education Initiative (EGEI)

The global context

The United Nations Girls' Education Initiative (UNGEI) was announced in April 2000 by the Secretary General of the United Nations at the World Education Forum in Dakar, Senegal. UNICEF was mandated to lead it. The Initiative called for everything that the Community Education movement in Egypt had been promoting, including intensified partnerships to improve girls' education. The Dakar Framework set clear gender-related goals and objectives for Education For All (EFA), which were later adopted as part of the Millennium Development Goals (MDGs) for education. They include eliminating the gender gap in primary and secondary education by 2005, and ensuring that by 2015 all children are in school, with parity and equality for girls and boys.

UNGEI represents a renewed commitment to achieve gender equality and reach the unmet MDG and EFA goals, by assuring girls of full and equal access to, and achievement in, basic education of good quality. It encourages countries to foster partnerships to attain these goals and to tackle gender issues in national plans of action, including sector plans and wider development frameworks. It motivates governments to take strategic action on girls' education, in a collaborative manner which develops known mechanisms and established practices. It calls for the building of flexible structures and – most importantly – strong partnerships which help to strengthen capacity to reach the goals and objectives of the global girls' education movement.

Renewed national commitment

In Egypt, a United Nations Education Task Force had been established in 2000, comprising UNICEF, UNDP, ILO, UNESCO, UNIFEM, UNFPA, and the World Bank. In October 2000, in a follow-up to the World Education Forum, this task force, led by UNICEF, brought together high-level policy makers in a national conference for girls' education. The National Council for Childhood and Motherhood (NCCM) was invited to play a prominent role, and the Ministry of Education was a strong partner. The Task Force thus created the conditions for a reinvigorated movement for girls' education in Egypt, continuing what had already been achieved, and responding to the renewed commitments made in Dakar.

The conference committed Egypt to the global UNGEI objectives. It reviewed studies which indicated that, while the country was doing well on national averages, wide disparities existed between and within regions, with a number of governorates identified as being at particularly great risk of failure. The conference recommended a focus on good-quality learning for all – marking a strategic shift away from a single focus on access – and also called for greater attention to early childhood care and development. An important series of recommendations focused on the creation of structures which would sustain the effort for girls' education in an integrated fashion. The need for a National Task Force and secretariat for girls' education was made explicit.

The National Task Force

In its capacity as co-ordinator with responsibility for children's welfare, the National Council for Childhood and Motherhood took on a leadership role at the national level. It set up a series of important advocacy events, attended by the First Lady of Egypt, who in fact presides over the council.

In partnership with UNICEF and the UN family, the council helped to create a national task force of 16 line ministries, several NGOs, and a number of government agencies. The task force was to create and strengthen a partnership between the different sectors and bring to the educational arena a comprehensive array of services to support girls' aspirations for education. Good health and nutrition were important components, identified as the responsibility of the Ministry of Health and Population. Income generation and poverty alleviation would be supported by the Ministry of Social Affairs, the Ministry of Youth, and the Social Fund for Development. The Ministry of Petroleum and the Ministry of Construction would provide roads. The Ministry of Environment was to provide materials and training on relevant issues related to environment and hygiene. Moral education was identified as the responsibility of the Ministry of Education and the Ministry of Religious Endowment. The Ministry of Culture proposed offering environment-friendly designs for the building of schools.

The above are just some examples of pledges made by the various partners during meetings of the National Task Force, and during meetings between the

First Lady and the member ministers. The foundation for an integrated approach has been laid.

Local task forces

A number of geographical areas with wide gaps between access for boys and access for girls had been selected for intensified action in seven governorates with the greatest disparities. Local voluntary task forces were created in these governorates, through a participatory process of rigorous consultations. Communities, parents, and members of civil society volunteered to form local teams/task forces. Girls, both in and out of school, were given the opportunity to participate. They were important members of the local task forces and played a significant role in the consultative processes. Women were also well represented in the voluntary task forces.

The self-selected local task forces, on average 20 in each governorate, were in fact viewed as the basis for community participation and were treated as key partners. Their capacity was gradually built through a series of training workshops on planning generally, and the development of action plans more specifically. As a result, they were able to produce action plans for each of the seven governorates. They were mentored and supported by planning experts, information committees, and budget committees from the ministries of finance, education, and planning. UNICEF supported the process and the finalisation of the plans. With some refinement, the outcomes of their endeavours led the government to earmark a budget of 157 million Egyptian pounds from the country's five-year plan, to be used specifically for girls' education. The actual cost of the initiative was a little more than threefold the amount allocated.

The local task forces were carefully trained in community mobilisation, selection of community leaders, and team building. As their teams are being strengthened, their terms of reference evolve. As the task forces develop into strong effective teams (through the on-going training), they will be the strongest partners of the initiative. They will be in charge of creating liaison officers and leaders at the district and village levels. They will, moreover, oversee the creation of education committees in all the targeted sites, basing them on the community school model.

It is the community partners in the initiative who will be selecting sites, facilitators/teachers, and students, and ultimately establishing girl-friendly schools in partnership with the official agencies responsible for school building. The model is essentially that of the community school, sharing its emphasis on the participation and empowerment of local communities and its characteristic classroom pedagogy and methodology of learning.

The work of the local task forces will be supported by the national task force, which will co-ordinate its efforts to provide the necessary technical assistance and executive resources. All the various ministries have made pledges to the First Lady to provide additional budgets and services to the initiative. Some private-sector entrepreneurs have donated cash and building materials. A significant media campaign accompanies the initiative, and public enthusiasm is high.

Local action plans

The action plans developed by the local task forces include programmes and projects on information systems, community mobilisation and advocacy, expansion of girl-friendly schools, and poverty alleviation. The plans aim to use innovative strategies to reach approximately half a million out-of-school girls in seven governorates. Two of the governorates, Assiut and Sohag, have well-developed community schools. Four of the selected governorates have already experimented with replications and variations of the community schools, namely One Classroom Schools and Small Schools. The innovative strategies to be introduced in all seven governorates would be as follows:

- the establishment of 3,000 additional girl-friendly schools;
- improvement of existing school environments;
- and improvements in the physical, social, and economic conditions of families and communities of out-of-school girls through service provision, income generation, and consciousness-raising activities.

Information systems would allow local communities to learn about and assist in collecting, entering, and analysing data. Members of local communities are in the best position to inform data collectors of the existence of communities in hard-to-reach areas which are normally unknown to official census staff. They will also feel empowered by sharing in the creation of information and having access to it. All the various strategies have already been piloted through the community school model.

Monitoring of the programmes would lie in the hands of the volunteer local task forces, under the guidance of the NCCM and in partnership with NGOs. A meticulously developed monitoring and evaluation plan will utilise numerous indicators for outputs, outcomes, and impacts of the activities in each of the projects and programmes. The plan was developed through a series of technical workshops organised by UNICEF. The local task forces will be trained in its use, with the objective of making the initiative accountable to the key stakeholders: the communities.

Training of facilitators and supervisors in the initiative is currently being conducted in accordance with tested pedagogies through the community school model. UNICEF gives technical support to the training. The approach is holistic, aiming to foster a constructive community of learners with a collective sense of responsibility to each other. The communities will take on leadership roles, and the power of partnerships should set in motion the wheels of a movement that has already registered significant gains (see Box 1).

The movement should ensure that girls will learn in an equitable way, within environments that are friendly and supportive of creativity, understanding, and critical thinking. It should also ensure that communities will learn about responsible participation. The empowerment of women, genuine respect for their latent abilities, and true democracy should also be fostered, as they were through the community schools.

Box 1: The Egypt Girls' Education Initiative: progress to date

A comprehensive vision has been developed for the initiative.

A special section for girls' education has been established in the five-year plan.

The sum of 157 million Egyptian pounds (US $26 million) has been earmarked for the initiative in the five-year plan (and an additional $80 million sought from the private sector and donors to support the initiative).

Relevant and effective structures have been established at the national level.

The National Task Force and the girls' education secretariat are fully operating at NCCM, with strong technical support from UNICEF and other UN agencies.

Local task forces have been set up as participatory mechanisms in the seven selected governorates; action plans in each of the governorates have been finalised through participatory processes, and information systems have been consolidated.

Capacity building and material support have been provided to local task forces and departments, and teachers and facilitators have been trained.

Several sites have been selected, according to rigorous criteria, for the creation of girl-friendly schools, and facilitators have been selected too.

The foundation stone for the first school was laid by the First Lady of Egypt in May 2003.

450 girl-friendly schools have been established.

On-going documentation of the initiative is underway.

Will the dream come true?

Realities are constructed out of a series of dreams that are made to come true; however, in this case the new realities need to be nurtured as they come into being, and there are many risks to be confronted.

Challenges to address

- The movement requires strong political commitment and a leadership which believes in the very essence of the development objectives sought. This currently exists in Egypt, as manifested by the leadership at NCCM. But the life of movements is long, and as they move through various phases they require continuous guidance and support. It is critical, therefore, that the political commitment and leadership are maintained over time. The infrastructure of innovation, reform, and democratic decision-making should be strong enough to support such a movement. This is gradually coming about, but will require sustained efforts in terms of mentoring and capacity building.

- For partnerships to be meaningful in any initiative, they need to be perceived as equitable by all the players involved. Historically, however, partnerships between officials and community members and leaders have been rather asymmetrical. Communities are assumed to be apolitical, while expected to contribute economically and socially. Allowing communities to be part of the planning and decision-making processes is an entirely new procedure. To sustain such initiatives and keep up the momentum, there is a need for intensive capacity building, coaching, mentoring, and training.

- Voluntary action has been most popular among the poorest of the poor, or alternatively as a matter for the individual philanthropist. In a political economy where general poverty prevails, it is often hard to sustain voluntary activity. But the local task forces in the Egypt Girls' Education Initiative have worked untiringly since they were established. They have a sense of pride and achievement, and their enthusiasm is growing. If successes continue to multiply, and recognition is strong, social capital should accumulate, enabling people to build strong community-based networks, based on trust.

- Forging partnerships between donors in very large initiatives requires a great deal of work. Fortunately, in Egypt the UN partner agencies have acted from a strong sense of collaboration and harmony. However, as the partnerships of necessity expand, much effort will be needed to ensure that this same spirit continues to prevail.

- Partnerships between line ministries that have hitherto often worked in complete isolation from each other will also require a high degree of co-ordination. Fortunately the First Lady in person is leading this process, thus making it hard for ministries to resist. The hope is that this current period of transition might lead to the internalisation of a crucial integrative process, which becomes the measure of success for the future. This will require mechanisms which allow for co-ordinated planning, together with clear responsibility and accountability.

- Another constraint will continue to be the need for sustained fundraising. The development phase of such a grand-scale initiative will require large sums of money. But the effort should pay off in the form of a wide range of long-term impacts. Although the government has financially supported a large part of the cost for the initiative, with contributions both in cash and in kind, an additional 80 million dollars will be needed over the period 2004–2007 to cover the costs. Fund-raising efforts are currently underway, supported by UNICEF.

- Finally, the complex nature of all the partnerships, and the very considerable effort needed to co-ordinate them, may impair the quality of the outcomes.

Despite such potential pitfalls and constraints, the dream is on the way to becoming reality, provided that it is continuously nurtured. This will call for sustained efforts on the part of NCCM, as an innovative government structure, to co-ordinate and lead the way forward in unconventional ways. It will furthermore require UNICEF, with the support of the UN family, to maintain its mediating role and support the cementing of partnerships between communities and government.

A continued role for UNICEF

From the beginning, UNICEF's role has consistently been that of a catalyst and mediator. It was a catalyst when initiating, designing, and assisting in the mainstreaming of the community school model which essentially established partnerships between various stakeholders so as to create good-quality learning opportunities for girls. It also mediated the relationship between government, communities, and NGOs when the model was scaled up, most notably through EGEI. It has assisted throughout in the formation of partnerships between essentially asymmetrical and often incompatible entities, which required official government institutions and bureaucrats to work alongside community members who were volunteers and aspired to be agents of change.

Such partnerships got off on the right footing when community members and leaders in fact took the lead in developing their own plans of action in the EGEI;

but the involvement of volunteers in such types of partnership requires conscious and sensitive negotiations and constant nurturing; in this, UNICEF has an important role to play in its capacity of mediator – which is a challenge, given its limited resources.

Building and monitoring the various partnerships has required work. Helping government officials to consider unconventional ideas has been no easy matter, especially since they were accustomed to vertical lines of authority, in a context within which each department or ministry worked separately. Moreover, it was no easy task to convince officials at the governorate levels that local task forces were to be recognised as legitimate bearers of girls' rights in their districts and villages; nor was it easy to persuade such officials to support community-based voluntary entities and accept them as equal partners. Finally, supporting volunteers to sustain their initial levels of enthusiasm requires intensive work and on-going communication.

It is important, therefore, that UNICEF and other international agencies understand the intensive demands on human resources that will be entailed if such movements are to be supported while they are scaled up in size and complexity. But the partnerships that are being developed in Egypt, at all the diversified levels of implementation, are helping to ensure that innovations continue to recreate themselves within government, communities, and civil society at large to achieve the best results. This in turn can only come about if international partnerships are fostered to contribute funding, technical assistance, and political support to initiatives such as these, which have the potential for positive social transformation.

Malak Zaalouk is chief of the education programme at UNICEF Cairo. She was the founder of the Community School movement in Egypt and she has been involved in the work of the UN Egypt Girls' Education Initiative since its inception.

Notes

1   The Canadian International Development Agency (CID), Project Support Unit (PSU): 'Community Education Project: End of Phase II Evaluation', June 2001.

2   National Center for Examination and Educational Evaluation, NCEEE: 'Evaluation of the Community Schools', Cairo, 2000.

8 Seeds of change: community alliances for girls' education

Lucy Lake and Angeline Mugwendere

The urgent case for girls' education has been unequivocally made. Over and above girls' right to education, there is now incontrovertible evidence demonstrating its profound and long-term benefits for improving health standards, stimulating economic activity, stabilising populations, and checking the spread of HIV/AIDS. At times, the magnitude of the problem of their exclusion from education means that the needs of individual girls themselves go unnoticed. Added to this is the problem of girls' silence: their plight has become an issue of global debate, in which the voices of young women themselves, particularly those in impoverished rural areas, are not heard. The challenge is to develop partnerships which can amplify the voice of girls and which can tap into a range of resources to address their needs, so that they can enrol and succeed in education. In this chapter we describe an innovative approach which is achieving just that, and we reflect on the potential for it to be scaled up, to change the lives of many thousands more girls who are currently denied the chance to go to school.

CAMFED (Campaign for Female Education) has been supporting girls' education since 1993. By 2003, we had enabled 56,208 girls to remain in school; 98 per cent were able to proceed to the next year of education. We work with rural communities to enable girls to go to school and then, as educated young women, to contribute to economic and social progress. Our focus is on girls in rural areas of sub-Saharan Africa, where more than 23 million girls are still out of school (UNESCO 2003). Our programmes currently operate in Zimbabwe, Zambia, and Ghana, where there are relatively well-developed education systems, thus offering opportunities for substantial qualitative improvement.

In Zimbabwe, where our work began, the initial focus of our programme was on the transition of girls from primary to secondary school, in recognition of the fact that the majority of girls were dropping out at this stage. Our aim was to challenge the then received wisdom that girls were not attending school because their families did not want their daughters to be educated. We set out to prove that when poverty-related constraints are removed, girls attend school alongside boys. In the process, we have found the greatest resource for girls' education to be parental and community concern for the welfare and future of their children.

We have also found that girls who complete school have a powerful role to play in extending educational opportunities to others: by being role models in their communities; by deepening local understanding of the problems affecting girls' school attendance; by enabling other children to claim their right to education, by meeting their school-going costs; and by campaigning at community, national, and international levels for an increase in the enrolment of girls.

The range and quality of partnerships developed by CAMFED have been critical to the programme's success. These alliances draw together all those who have an influence over girls' lives, from their families and communities to national and international policy makers, in order to tackle the range of problems that limit girls' educational success. Significantly, the partnerships now include young women who have completed school and who are collaborating with parents and local authorities, including patriarchal chiefs, to demand better education for all children from local and national policy-making bodies. These alliances are now at the vanguard of the spread of the programme to new communities and to new countries; partnerships are being set up between communities to promote the exchange of good practice and enable even the most impoverished communities to understand from the direct experience of others how it is possible to fulfil their aspirations to educate their children.

The virtuous cycle of girls' education

In this section, we describe the basis of the partnerships that we develop: by placing girls at the centre of concern, CAMFED builds local understanding of the constraints on girls' access, retention, and success at school. The result is a 'virtuous cycle', illustrated in Figure 1, through which CAMFED enables girls to complete school and move on to become leaders of change in their communities.

Economic empowerment of parents

We begin from the premise that poverty is the underlying cause of girls' exclusion, which must be addressed as the principal constraint if more girls are to enrol in school. We do so by providing the financial resources to pay girls' school-going costs, such as fees, clothing, and stationery. By enabling groups of girls to attend their local schools, the issue of girls' education is brought into local focus. By tracking these groups on their journey through education, we are able to identify and address the pitfalls that girls face at crucial transition points – in moving from primary to secondary education, for example – when other factors, such as increased distance to school, become critical. Additionally, the

Figure 1: The virtuous cycle of girls' education

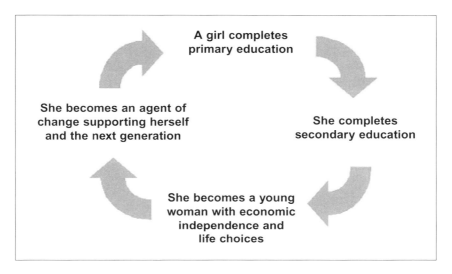

peer support implicit within these groups, combined with the increased self-esteem among girls as a result of the attention paid to their welfare, serves to amplify their voices so that we can bring previously unacknowledged or misunderstood problems to the centre of concern. These include sensitive and often hidden problems which can have a serious impact on girls' retention and success at school, such as the lack of sanitary wear, which discourages regular school attendance. The cost of conventional sanitary wear in Zimbabwe has caused many girls to resort to the use of unsafe alternatives, such as old cloths or bark, or it has forced them to stay away from school for the duration of menstruation. At a recent community workshop, attended by more than 150 parents, local government officials, teachers and students, one child shared her story and reduced many listeners to tears with the realisation of what she had endured.

Sinikiwe (not her real name) is sixteen years old. She is in Form 4 at a local secondary school. Her mother died two years ago. She lives with her grandmother and two younger brothers and sister. Sinikiwe told how for the past two years she had missed class every month because she did not have any sanitary protection. In addition, there were many days when she had to leave school early, to take care of her grandmother or younger siblings when they were unwell. This meant that she missed school for an average of five days every month, and thus missed 15 to 20 days of schooling per term. By the end of the year this amounted to 60 days (two full months). Already, she was at a severe disadvantage in the classroom in relation to her male peers.

Sinikiwe's story illustrates how poverty can have a far greater impact on the education of girls than on that of boys. Easing the financial burden on poor families by paying girls' school-going costs reduces the pressure which might otherwise force parents to take decisions that would ultimately undermine their daughters' education. Without such support, some single mothers might take life-threatening risks by resorting to commercial sex work in a desperate attempt to secure food, clothing, and school fees for their children; girls will drop out of school to relieve the burden of school fees from their families; some will be forced into early marriage in times of drought, to secure a bride-price that will guarantee the survival of their families until the next season.

The provision of financial support acknowledges the struggle that families endure to ensure the well-being of their children. CAMFED recognises that financial resources are not the sole factor that will enable girls to remain in school and succeed, but that they are a crucial initial input. With the immediate pressure on them lifted, families have more time and opportunity to consider the other inputs that are needed for their daughters to complete school successfully. CAMFED then uses this opportunity to create a forum for learning and action on girls' education, with the full participation of impoverished and marginalised families, who are now freed up to contribute. Their participation is vital to the design of any further interventions to improve girls' education, because such families have the greatest knowledge of the poverty-related constraints that need to be addressed. The economic empowerment of parents is also vital if they are to join with community authorities to make demands on the school system, and ultimately to demand greater access and better education for all. Otherwise, locked in a daily struggle for survival, they would have no time or energy for any but the most tokenistic representation in wider campaigns.

Economic independence for school leavers

Girls who successfully complete school, particularly where they are in a minority, have the potential to become important role models in their communities and galvanise wide support for girls' education. For this to happen, however, the issue of post-school opportunities for girls must be addressed. This brings us to the third stage of the 'virtuous cycle' in the CAMFED programme. Girls who complete school face high expectations from their families and communities which, if unfulfilled, can have a detrimental impact – both on the girls themselves and on the wider cause of girls' education, as there is a risk that their schooling might be written off as a 'wasted' investment. Confronted with the expectation that they will find formal employment on completing school and bring income to their families, many young women leave the rural areas in search of work in towns, where they are extremely vulnerable to economic and sexual exploitation. As a result, their potential is lost to their communities, and this in turn is a serious disincentive for communities to unite around supporting more girls to go to school, not least because of the fear of what will become of their daughters.

The long-term benefits of girls' education are often not apparent until the next generation when, as future mothers, educated women are likely to have fewer, healthier children, who are in turn more likely to go to school. In the short term, however, these benefits may be invisible to many people in communities that are trapped in a daily struggle for survival. Much more immediate evidence is needed if families and communities are to be inspired to invest their limited resources in enabling more girls to go to school, and if a momentum of change for the current generation of girls is to be achieved.

The issue of post-school opportunities for girls thus needs to be addressed alongside activities to improve their school retention and success. While at first glance this may seem a daunting challenge, CAMFED has found that when strong community partnerships have been forged to promote the cause of girls' education, these partnerships can help to extend the problem-solving process to cover post-school opportunities. In the CAMFED programme, this has been attempted by working with local authorities to support school-leavers who are unable to progress to further education or employment, creating opportunities for them to start small-scale businesses. This has involved designing a micro-finance scheme which specifically targets the needs of young rural women who, in their own words, 'have never before handled more money than is needed to buy a packet of salt', and who lack the collateral to guarantee a loan – a fact which excludes them from more conventional credit schemes. This has not been an easy process: it involves challenging received wisdom concerning young women's capabilities, and continuing to build their confidence and skills so that they can themselves rebuff criticism and opposition, by the example of their own achievements.

Two key features which underpin the success of this scheme are the peer support and mentoring between the young entrepreneurs, which extends from their peer groups at school and results from the policy of supporting girls to attend in groups; and the support, guidance, and training provided by the community authorities who originally united with CAMFED in partnership to promote the education of these young women. In Zimbabwe, more than 300 successful rural businesses have been set up by young women school-leavers over the past three years. The young women's new-found economic status, combined with the social confidence acquired through their education, has propelled them into a position from which they can now join with community authorities and campaign for better education for the younger generation. The 'virtuous cycle' is complete.

Community alliances

In this section, we describe the community alliances that CAMFED forges which support the successful completion of the 'virtuous cycle' and generate a wider momentum for change within communities. The first step in establishing these alliances is to work with communities to use their power to support girls' education. This involves identifying key constituencies, responding to their doubts and scepticism, and drawing them into a forum to examine the problems that girls face and explore their collective potential to solve them.

Establishing district committees

At the centre of this forum is a district-level committee, set up by CAMFED with responsibility for mobilising and distributing resources. Such committees create an alliance of people who have an influence on girls' lives; they include representation from local government authorities, traditional leaders, parents, police, schools, the health service, and non-government agencies. Where girls have successfully completed school, the committee also includes school 'graduates'. In drawing their membership from a broad cross-section of the community, the committees acquire a wide perspective, and consequently a degree of authority, on the question of girls' education. Significantly, the committees include patriarchal authorities, such as chiefs, as a way of acknowledging that the education of girls is central to community welfare and development as a whole.

Building community confidence

At the outset, CAMFED makes a commitment to support groups of local girls to attend school. It initiates a dialogue within the community, to discuss how to identify the girls in greatest need, and how to support them to attend their local schools. This commitment to action by CAMFED is vital to inspire reciprocal involvement by communities, which is evidenced by the fact that the relatively small injection of finance needed for groups of girls in a community to enrol in school unlocks a wealth of local in-kind resources on which the programme can draw to address wider problems affecting girls' school retention, such as the use of local transport to facilitate school visits to monitor girls' welfare; the provision of psycho-social support to girls by local women; and the contribution of time and knowledge by local people to tackle the problems. The value that CAMFED places on these contributions is crucial to building community confidence and inspiring a wider commitment to change.

The balance of power within the committees is sought in the first place by virtue of the broad representation of local constituencies. CAMFED then acts as facilitator to help to negotiate power relations between the various groups. A key objective is to ensure that groups who are traditionally marginalised, including impoverished rural parents and girls, have a strong voice on the committees and participate fully in decisions about the distribution of resources, so that they are not further disempowered through token representation. This involves extensive capacity building of these groups by CAMFED, and the development of systems of local accountability for the use of resources which are widely accessible and understood. The obstacles are considerable, and the pace at times is slow, but the achievements of this process are evident in examples of the growing representation of rural women in school-governance bodies, and invitations from chiefs to young women to speak at community gatherings and even to act as facilitators in traditional courts.

Resolving tensions

Membership of the committees is voluntary, and no allowances are paid out. Thus, it is those people who are genuinely committed to change who become (and remain)involved. This is not always the case: there can be antagonism over the perceived resources involved, and respect between constituency groups is hard won. The way in which such differences are resolved is very important. CAMFED sets in place key incentives to inspire commitment, including the principle of ensuring that resources reach the communities for whom they are intended, and are not diverted into layers of organisational bureaucracy and costly overheads. CAMFED also ensures that people are rewarded in kind for their contribution: in the opportunity to represent their case at national level, to try out new ways to solve local problems, and to travel to learn from other communities and organisations. This is not to say that problems have not been encountered in the development of the committees, but what gives the programme its real strength is the manner in which these problems are solved. To give an example: in one district, a local councillor attempted to exploit the process through which girls were identified for support, by nominating individuals according to the political affiliation of their families. To resolve the issue, an experienced team, including a senior chief and councillor from a neighbouring district where the programme had been in place for some years, facilitated a meeting between the committee and local parents, at which the principles for identifying girls were reconsidered and agreed. Through this process of peer-to-peer mentoring, CAMFED acknowledges and endorses the knowledge and expertise of those involved in the frontline of the programme.

Addressing threats to girls' health and safety

The resulting strong alliances have enabled problems to be solved across a broad front. One example is that of addressing the issue of travel from home to school, a seemingly intractable problem in impoverished and remote areas, where boarding places would put the cost of education beyond the means of local families, and where low population density negates the possibility of establishing additional schools. Community alliances in Zimbabwe, Zambia, and Ghana have found a solution to this problem. They have mobilised local resources to establish community hostels, where girls can live in safety near school during term-time. In the Nyaminyami district of Zimbabwe, where the first such hostel was established in 1997, the on-going costs are now entirely sustained locally. The pride in the success of this achievement has strengthened community confidence to tackle other desperate problems, including the effects of HIV/AIDS, and the community is now considering how this model can be adapted to address another growing concern: that of care for children orphaned by AIDS. The Nyaminyami community is also now presenting the hostel as a model to representatives from other districts facing similar problems, and has hosted international agencies to share lessons from the project and explore the potential for its replication.

An important benefit of the community alliances is that they unite different authorities and overcome bureaucratic hurdles to their co-operation. This is vital for addressing the wide range of issues relating to girls' education, including problems of their health and safety in the school and wider community. The fact that young women have now joined these alliances means that local authorities benefit from the perspective of girls and young women, a fact which is deepening their understanding of the problems that girls face, and helping them to respond in the most appropriate and effective manner. This has enabled some of the most sensitive issues to be brought to the surface, most notably the problem of sexual abuse. Some community alliances are promoting collective understanding of the extent of abuse and its impact, as well as facilitating joint action to tackle it. Young women in Zimbabwe are, for example, now able to engage with local authorities to take up cases of abuse uncovered during their work with girls; parents are able to approach school authorities to address the issue of the safety of their daughters in school; and chiefs are co-operating with the judiciary and Ministry of Education to punish the perpetrators and introduce bye-laws to protect girls more effectively. The result is a campaign against abuse across communities in Zimbabwe which is now being heard at national level. This has not been an easy plateau to reach, but meticulous attention to the detail of the relationships between the various stakeholders that influence girls' education has paid huge dividends.

The multiplier effect

'The multiplier effect' refers to the impact in communities where young women have completed school and become leading agents of change: the final phase in the virtuous cycle. These young women are uniting to extend educational opportunities to children in their communities, inspiring others to join them, and enabling the voices of rural girls and young women to be heard at the national and international levels.

The process by which girls have been supported through school in the CAMFED programme, a process which engages their communities, means that the success of these girls in completing school is a source of collective pride and celebration. This creates the crucial basis for young women to be able to move on from school to join community alliances and ultimately work hand-in-hand with local authorities to expand educational opportunities for other girls.

CAMA: a support network for young women activists

These young women have set up CAMA, the CAMFED Association, a support network for young women school leavers which aims to unite them in a common goal to eradicate poverty in their communities. CAMA was first established in 1998 in Zimbabwe, followed by the launch of a sister network in Ghana in 2002. In Zimbabwe, CAMA's membership currently numbers 2,000, extending across 14 districts of the country. This membership is growing, and CAMA has recently opened the opportunity to all young women school leavers committed to becoming activists in their communities. CAMA is governed by a network of district and national committees, elected bi-annually by the membership, and is supported by a team of national and international advisers with experience in the field of grassroots women's movements.

CAMA uses the rural school network as the focal point for all its activities, capitalising on the strong partnerships with schools and local authorities developed over the course of CAMFED's programme of support for girls' education. CAMA members now provide mentoring to girls in schools, and are operating a community health programme to share information on HIV/AIDS, reaching more than 95,000 children during 2003. Such is local authorities' respect for these young women that they are being invited to participate in decision-making bodies and are being consulted by local authorities, including police and chiefs, in cases involving girls and young women in the community.

Perhaps most significantly, CAMA members are using their own early experience of exclusion, and the transformative potential of education, to extend this opportunity to other girls in their communities. CAMA members are themselves now supporting other children to attend school, and are reaching children who are desperately vulnerable, including those orphaned by AIDS. They are doing so both by raising funds as an association, and by using their own personal income, including the profits that they generate from their rural businesses, to support more children to go to school. They are also raising in-kind support from communities, for example the donation of second-hand clothes to provide girls with decent school-wear. The fact that CAMA members were once themselves in a position of exclusion from education means that they understand its psychological impact and, alongside the provision of material support, can work with orphaned and vulnerable children to confront the psycho-social problems that may prevent their retention and success at school. Figure 2 illustrates the impact that CAMA is already having, and the numbers of children that CAMA members are reaching.

The success of CAMA is underpinned by the community alliances that were forged by CAMFED to promote girls' education. The alliances have created the platform for girls to complete school and move on to become powerful advocates and activists on behalf of other vulnerable children. These young women are now the ambassadors for girls' education at the community level, and are beginning to take up similar positions on the national and international stages. They represent a new and potentially powerful constituency which will increasingly demand tangible results for girls and their families from the massive international investment that is being allocated to girls' education.

Scaling up the achievements of community alliances

The community alliances set up to support girls' education, which now include the young women who have completed school, have the greatest knowledge of the problems of girls' exclusion from school, because they confront these problems daily. They also now possess the experience, expertise, and confidence to solve them, and they represent in theory the most effective vehicle for scaling up CAMFED's approach, with the aim of achieving the 'multiplier effect' in many more communities.

By establishing links between communities across Africa, these alliances could mobilise even the most marginalised communities, by inspiring them with evidence of what can be achieved even in the face of apparently intractable problems. While the details of the problems may vary between communities, the principles which determine the problem-solving process could be replicated to achieve change on behalf of girls. Cost-effectiveness and sustainability are intrinsic to this approach to scaling up, by virtue of the fact that it can mobilise local resources and build community confidence to continue the process of change.

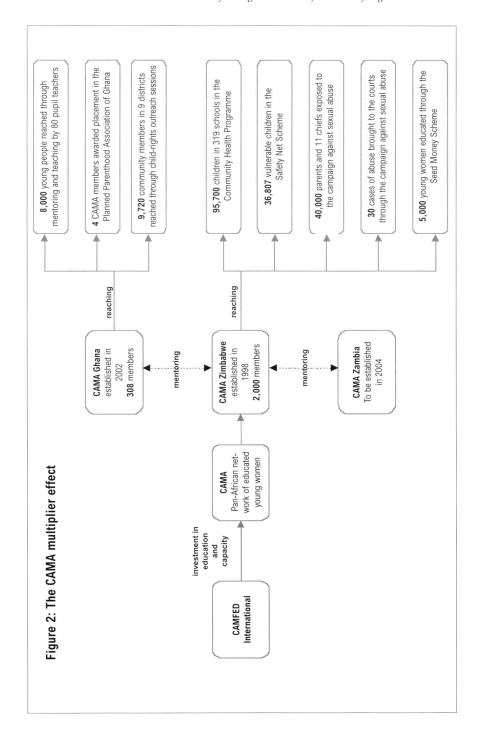

Figure 2: The CAMA multiplier effect

CAMFED International

investment in education and capacity

CAMA
Pan-African net-work of educated young women

CAMA Ghana
established in 2002
308 members

mentoring

CAMA Zimbabwe
established in 1998
2,000 members

mentoring

CAMA Zambia
To be established in 2004

reaching

reaching

8,000 young people reached through mentoring and teaching by 80 pupil teachers

4 CAMA members awarded placement in the Planned Parenthood Association of Ghana

9,720 community members in 9 districts reached through child-rights outreach sessions

95,700 children in 319 schools in the Community Health Programme

36,807 vulnerable children in the Safety Net Scheme

40,000 parents and 11 chiefs exposed to the campaign against sexual abuse

30 cases of abuse brought to the courts through the campaign against sexual abuse

5,000 young women educated through the Seed Money Scheme

This process of extending community alliances across Africa has already begun. Communities are being linked in Zimbabwe, Zambia, and Ghana. Peer-mentoring is taking place between local chiefs, school authorities, and girls. In the case of Zambia, the process was initiated in 2001, when a team from Zimbabwe, representative of the alliances and including a chief, a district education officer, a councillor, a head teacher, a parent, and a CAMA member, presented the approach to the Ministry of Education and its partners. The concept received the ministry's full support. Links were established with communities in three provinces, and a lively exchange is underway with communities in Zimbabwe, resulting in widespread efforts to improve girls' retention in school beyond the early years of basic education. These alliances are beginning to provide communities with an important means of addressing the complex problems that impede girls' education.

A crucial ingredient for the successful extension of community alliances to new areas and new countries is the participation of the young women who have completed school as a result of community efforts. They are important role models who represent the immediate and tangible evidence of the benefits of supporting girls' education. Their success inspires and draws in those people who are genuinely committed to extend educational opportunities to more girls. Another critical factor is the broadly representative nature of the teams that lead and monitor the programme's introduction to new communities, and which include government, civil authorities, and school authorities, as well as parents and school-leavers. These teams can identify and address local power dynamics, engage the most marginalised groups in decision making, and ensure that best practice is developed in the management of resources to promote local transparency and accountability.

The greatest obstacle to this approach to scaling up lies with the international community, which does not yet recognise the immense untapped potential within rural communities to solve the problem of girls' educational exclusion. Donors need to have faith in the capabilities of impoverished communities to manage substantial resources to achieve this goal. This shift is crucial if the massive resources being channelled into the field of girls' education are genuinely to achieve change for the current generation of girls.

We hope that in this chapter we have made the case for girls' education even more urgent, both by highlighting the commitment that exists in rural communities, and by demonstrating that young educated women have a powerful role to play in extending educational opportunities for the current generation of children. To some readers, this may seem impossibly idealistic, but the rapidity with which this approach is taking root, and the demands for its introduction by other communities, indicates the opportunity for wide-scale change. We end with the voice of one young woman who represents this potential: Fiona Muchembere, once herself excluded from education by her family's poverty, is a CAMA member and newly qualified lawyer in Zimbabwe, now fighting for girls' education and lobbying for changes in legislation to improve girls' welfare in school:

> *We now have freedom in every sphere of life, economic freedom through professions and enterprise, and reproductive freedom in deciding when to marry, who to marry and when to have a child. This in itself is breaking the vicious cycle of poverty. This is the message that we bring to you, so that you can realise the potential that is in a rural girl who, when given a chance, can do wonders for her family and community.*

Lucy Lake is Programme Director of CAMFED International. She joined CAMFED in 1994 and over the past ten years has worked to develop a range of practical initiatives to promote girls' educational opportunities. This has included the establishment of CAMA as a representative voice for African girls and young women.

Angeline Mugwendere is the Director of CAMA, the CAMFED Association, a movement of young rural women in Zimbabwe, Zambia, and Ghana, dedicated to promoting girls' education in Africa. Angeline founded CAMA in 1998 in Zimbabwe, along with a group of young women from rural areas who had completed school with the support of CAMFED.

Further reading

Cotton, Ann (2003) 'CAMFED's Philosophy and Practice: A Briefing Paper', EFA Monitoring Report, Paris, UNESCO.

Conclusion

Nitya Rao and Ines Smyth

This book has followed two parallel but connected lines. One examines the complexities associated with forging effective and sustainable partnerships among development actors with differing agendas. The other reflects on the potential impact of such endeavours on the promotion of girls' education and, more broadly, gender-equitable education, in the context of the Millennium Development Goals. To conclude, we summarise here the central themes of the preceding chapters, with particular emphasis on the lessons to be learned if the MDGs for education are indeed to be achieved.

In current international development discourse, partnerships are seen as the way forward. A document entitled '"Last Call for 2005": Consensus Statement of UNGEI (The UN Girls' Education Initiative) to the High Level Group', produced in October 2003, prioritised the need to 'scale up efforts by strengthening and expanding partnerships that ensure sustainable outcomes' and 'strengthen existing synergies that focus on gender equity goals' as key action points.

Using examples from a range of partnerships in various contexts, contributors to this book have argued that partnerships for girls' education operate in many guises and forms. There is diversity both between and within partnerships in terms of ideologies, scale, intentions, and achievements. The examples offered here illustrate that, rather than being static, the relationships that bind partners together undergo transformations. Rather than assuming, therefore, that partnerships take a universal, standard form, or even that they are uniformly positive, it is important to develop a more contextualised and nuanced understanding.

Power relations, flexibility, and sustainability

The case studies in this book show that to understand partnerships we must take into account, above all, power relations between different groups and institutions in society, as well as the processes by which those can be negotiated to meet particular purposes.

Different actors have their own priorities and approaches. To achieve a shared goal, certain conditions appear to be key. One is the need for clarity of purpose and roles at different levels, so that relative power and strengths, experiences, and resources are recognised and maximised for a common purpose. Achieving such clarity of purpose should be made easier by the existence of the Millennium Development Goals. Of the latter, the most pertinent are **Goal 2: Achieve Universal Primary Education**, with the target of ensuring that '*by 2015, children everywhere, boys and girls alike, will be able to complete a full course of primary schooling*'; and **Goal 3: Promote Gender Equality and Empower Women**, with the target of '*Eliminating gender disparity in primary and secondary education, preferably by 2005, and at all levels of education no later than 2015*'. These goals and targets have prompted debates which question whether they are relevant and realistic, and whether the processes of consultation are adequate to achieve them.

A civil-society e-discussion (14 June–5 July 2004) about the Millennium Project Task Force report on Education and Gender Equality identified several concerns. Perhaps the toughest question is this: *Is gender parity in access to education sufficient either to promote gender-equitable education or to contribute to women's empowerment?* There was consensus among the participants on the need to extend the gender-equality goal from education to other areas of life, including reproductive health, infrastructure provision, property rights, discrimination in labour markets, representation in political bodies, and sexual and gender-based violence, because together these wider strategies can contribute to the empowerment of women.

Such debates also demand a stronger reliance on existing commitments such as the Convention on the Elimination Of All Forms of Discrimination Against Women (CEDAW) and the Beijing Platform for Action, ratified by the international community, which make connections between critical issues for girls and women such as poverty, ill health, violence, armed conflict, and poor provision of education and training. The other question to be asked, then, is this: *What are we campaigning for: is it equal access to education for girls and boys (gender parity) or changes in education which will allow them all to obtain the maximum benefits in terms of learning and self-development (gender equality)?*

The e-discussion centred on the particular framing of the strategies, with some participants urging the need to stay true to *gendered* strategies (not merely those focused on girls and women). Others argued against shifting the MDG from primary to secondary education, noting, in the words of one correspondent, that 'by shifting the agenda upwards to secondary schooling and outwards to other gender equality issues, we risk losing or over-stretching the powerful consensus that underpins the MDGs'. Some participants argued that the main justification for secondary education appears to be framed in terms of its economic outcomes, whereas it is important not to forget the intrinsic value of education: the confidence, self-assurance, and skills that learners gain from even a little schooling can change their lives. Recognising that education is a holistic process, and that all levels, from primary to adult, are important, the participants in the discussion emphasised, however, the importance of not abandoning the missed gender-parity goal, but rather using the opportunity to galvanise action to meet this target – which is an essential element of all attempts to reform other levels of education.

The diversity of opinions reflected in this e-debate, as well as in the chapters of this book, demonstrates that flexibility is another precondition for the success of partnerships. Flexibility may require that actors in partnerships surrender their individual identity, if only temporarily, and work towards a mutually negotiated plan. Rivalry for space and profile in national and international forums, competition between the claims of different groups (girls and boys, students and teachers, etc.), and competing claims for legitimate interventions (formal versus non-formal education) must be put aside, because they are counterproductive.

The case studies in this book show that the success of partnership depends on both the nature of partnerships and the types of organisation that create the relationship. Loose alliances generally tend to work better than tight, bureaucratic arrangements. Partnerships which bring together organisations with similar ideologies and visions tend to work best. In the context of the Millennium Development Goals and targets, it will be important to put such lessons into practice: for example, by exploring the commonality of purpose which undoubtedly exists between organisations interested in education on the one hand, and women's groups on the other. The women's movement, broadly understood, has a wealth of experience and knowledge which must be harnessed more systematically to support progress towards gender-equitable education – both as an end in itself, and as a means of achieving gender equality. It is crucial to recognise that not all the partnerships presented here have assumed the promotion of girls' education or gender-equitable education as their primary (or even secondary) goal. It cannot be expected that networks and alliances will be entirely re-forged on the basis of a new purpose, different from that which brought them together in the first place. However, the reality of gender disparities in all aspects of education would appear sufficient reason for flexible partnerships and for many relevant organisations (the anti-globalisation movement, environmental campaigns, anti-debt coalitions, etc.) to reconsider their aims, if not their overall focus. They have in the past displayed creativity and imagination which could serve well the goal of gender-equitable education.

Partnerships that are characterised by great imbalances of power – such as those established between the State and small NGOs engaged in innovative programmes – carry considerable risks, including the possibility that the less powerful partners will become assimilated and lose their identity. But such collaborations have the potential also to be extremely effective. Small organisations are often more careful than big ones, when implementing innovative programmes, to ensure that lessons are learned from them. Larger, more powerful bodies must have the foresight to invest in smaller groups and to ensure that their innovations can be scaled up in a sustainable manner. Northern-based coalitions must learn to develop positions and ways of working which reflect the priorities of Southern members, and their greater human and financial resources must be placed at the disposal of the latter.

Our examples also show – ironically, yet not surprisingly – that poor communities, and within them certain groups (such as indigenous people, girls themselves, and children living in conflict), are still not always recognised as legitimate and active partners in coalitions that are supposed to benefit them. The goal of Education For All is achievable if communities and relevant groups 'own' such initiatives. This requires longer-term programmes, addressing local needs and constraints, and building local capacities – rather than implementing hurriedly conceived one-off projects. Further, there is the paradox that national goals and targets cannot be achieved without centralised planning and implementation – but sustainable outcomes cannot be achieved without flexibility and sensitivity to local conditions.

Leadership, resources, and accountability

Another lesson, perhaps the most obvious, is the necessity for all partners, and especially the best-endowed, to invest resources of time, funds, and people in the partnership, and to nurture it by supporting innovative initiatives, replicating good practice, and providing strong overall leadership.

The e-debate discussed above drew attention to the weakness of international partnerships, whether the MDGs, or Education For All, or the Fast-Track Initiative, which have failed to mobilise sufficient technical and financial resources to meet their goals. The allocation of resources by both governments and international agencies must be done equitably, to ensure justice particularly for excluded groups, which include girls and women in most countries. Educating girls strengthens women's voice in the community and stimulates social change. So continued support is needed in order to improve the quality of formal schooling (PROBE 1999), but also essential are well-designed and long-term initiatives to support adult literacy and non-formal education programmes for adolescents, to give another chance to those who have dropped out of school.

Recent transformations in the structure and working of UNGEI promise a new level of engagement by important partners. The Partnership on Sustainable Strategies for Girls' Education, described by Igboemeka in this collection, has now been merged with UNGEI. While this is undoubtedly a move towards harmonisation and improved co-ordination, it increases the expectation that UNGEI, and UNICEF, which is leading it, will adopt a stronger and more explicit gender perspective, retaining a commitment to promote girls' education when appropriate, alongside the more comprehensive aim of 'gender-equitable education'.

It is to be hoped also that UNGEI will lobby the World Bank to ensure that its Fast Track Initiative (a key mechanism to mobilise resources) will place more emphasis on gender-equitable education. While there was a passing reference to gender equality in the original FTI framework, and there is some later reference to gender-disaggregated analysis, including gender-specific monitoring indicators, these have not yet been confirmed.

In the new climate of increased accountability, all such initiatives should be regularly scrutinised for their commitments and achievements in terms of promoting girls' education and gender-equitable education. Apart from the existing indicators, new tools, designed to assess quality and accountability, are available for use. Examples are the 'scorecard' and the 'gender-empowerment measure' developed by the Beyond Access Project: Gender, Education, and Development, co-ordinated by Oxfam GB and the Institute of Education at London University. The scorecard, measuring girls' net attendance rate at primary school, girls' retention rate over five years in primary school, girls' secondary net enrolment ratio, and a country's gender development index (GDI), goes beyond gender parity to show how access and retention are part of a progression towards gender equity in society (Unterhalter et al. 2004). Similarly, the gender empowerment measure is a weighted index, which includes the following criteria:

- the proportion of women in decision-making positions in education
- women as a percentage of total head teachers in primary and secondary schools
- the ratio of estimated incomes of women and men as teachers and other workers in education and in other sectors
- and the proportion of education budget spent on specific measures to promote gender equity in education (such as strategies to counter sexual violence in schools).

Acting as a watchdog, monitoring progress, and demanding accountability is thus another important dimension of partnerships, apart from direct engagement in the formulation and implementation of education policy.

Finally, it is important that partners in any joint endeavour should work not towards the 'lowest common denominator', in the words of Tomasevski (2003), but to the highest standards and broadest visions. Even the MDGs – perhaps the most ambitious exercise in goal-setting ever attempted in development – do not, in the opinion of the Women's Environment and Development Organization, 'represent the full vision of gender equity, equality, and women's empowerment or poverty eradication and structural transformation envisioned in key human rights instruments' (WEDO 2004: 4).

We now know that the deadline for a key target – *the elimination of gender disparities in primary and secondary education by 2005* – has been missed, yet this is not a reason to abandon partnerships for girls' education. Rather, it should be the impetus for renewing and revitalising them, to ensure that the 2015 deadlines will be met.

References

Summary of e-discussion on Gender Equality MDG and Task Force Report, accessed from www.dgroups.org/groups/Right2education

PROBE (1999) *Public Report on Basic Education in India*, New Delhi: Oxford University Press.

Unterhalter, E., E. Kioko-Echessa, R. Pattman, R. Rajagopalan, and F. N'Jai (2004) 'Scaling Up Girls' Education: Towards a Scorecard on Girls' Education in the Commonwealth', Beyond Access Project, London: Institute of Education and Oxfam GB.

WEDO (2004) *Women's Empowerment, Gender Equality, and the Millennium Development Goals: A WEDO Information and Action Guide*, New York: Women's Environment and Development Organization.

Index